T0209007

CATHERINE SAMPSON

BETWEEN THE IRONS

Anecdotes of my life with horses

iUniverse, Inc.
Bloomington

iUniverse books may be ordered through booksellers or by contacting:

iUniverse
1663 Liberty Drive
Bloomington, IN 47403
www.iuniverse.com
1-800-Authors (1-800-288-4677)

Because of the dynamic nature of the Internet, any Web addresses or links contained in this book may have changed since publication and may no longer be valid. The views expressed in this work are solely those of the author and do not necessarily reflect the views of the publisher, and the publisher hereby disclaims any responsibility for them.

ISBN: 978-1-4502-6092-3 (sc)
ISBN: 978-1-4502-6093-0 (ebook)

Printed in the United States of America

iUniverse rev. date: 12/10/2010

For fifty-five years, my mother, Barbara Hosken (née Payne), supported my dreams and aspirations, giving healthy advice as only one who had lived through a struggling existence could. The Great Depression and World War II clicked at her heels, burrowing scars deep within her character. Those hard years and others in her life gave my mother a steely strength and courage. Although she often told people that I was the strongest person she ever knew, if that is true, then I inherited her tenacity.

She listened to my grievances, hopes, and goals and always had a positive and wise word of encouragement. She was my inspiration for writing this book and was instrumental in witnessing the past and reflecting on those memories that were a part of my family roots from which I could draw in my writings. I dedicate this book of my life to her honour. I was blessed to have had such a devoted mother in whose spirit I will go forward into an unknown world of intrigue, danger, and passion, laced with a hearty laugh.

In the shadow of a horse, our souls are nourished with humility and compassion.

Table of Contents

Acknowledgments

I wish to acknowledge those individuals in my life who have been instrumental in pointing my compass in the right direction. It has given me pause to reflect on their wisdom and influence they have shared with me throughout this epic journey. They have made a profound impact on my life.

Robert, my husband of 31 years, has put up with my driven passion for horses. He has been my best friend and supporter of my dream to breed Morgan horses, train and teach others. Without his constant love, patience and assistance, this may never have been accomplished.

My family has been my anchor and safe harbour throughout my life. Although they do not share this craziness for horses, they accept and admire my determination to follow my destiny.

I would also like to recognize the wonderful contributions to my early equine education by the late Elzier Pigeau. His quiet hands and encouraging voice gave me the confidence to try.

For more than three decades, Dr Harry Morrison has been my healer of horses and friend. His unwavering devotion to horses and genuine love of the species is duly noted in his work with these magnificent animals. I owe him a debt of gratitude more than money could ever suffice.

Lastly, I would like to thank the public who have believed in me and my work with horses. It is for them that this book was written.

Preface

It has been a long time since I first swung a leg over a pony and sat gingerly in the creaking leather of a Western saddle. What a thrill it was to actually be atop these noble creatures. The beginner rider had arrived. I would fill the pages of my little pink diary for several years. Most entries included references to horses and other animals of some sort.

As the decades passed and the memories lingered, I was prodded by friends and clients to put these passages in my life to paper.

Born in the small town of North Bay, Ontario, I still consider myself a northerner although I have lived most of my life in the south. Far from the haunting calls of the loon and wolf, the south has provided me with a different set of skills and opportunities to work, train, and show horses on a national scale.

For close to four decades, I have been involved with my favourite breed of horse since childhood, the Morgan. I owned my very first purebred Morgan when I was twenty-one. The little colt I had chosen to raise and train as a project of sorts established the cornerstone of a breeding program that would attain international status. Countless champions would follow as a result of these meagre beginnings with one special stallion. Today, well over 1,000 ribbons adorn the arena walls as a constant reminder of how far we have come. There is a story of struggle, faith, and commitment behind every ribbon on that wall. That little piece of satin that hung from a bridle is not to honour the lowly rider. Instead, it is to honour the horse for its performance and ultimate devotion to its rider's will. Every ribbon earned, regardless of colour, should be cherished. If not a ribbon, a gentle pat of thanks to the horse will suffice. It is not the rider that the public sees; it is ultimately the horse in all its glory.

My involvement with the Morgan breed earned me two terms as president of the local provincial Morgan club, and I have held directorships for many years. My husband and I have been honoured by the American Morgan Horse Association with bronze, silver, and gold medallions for breed promotion. We have also seen recognition from the Canadian Morgan Horse Association. Still, it is not the large crowds at demonstrations and parades or accolades from the show arena while grasping silver hardware and flowers of victory, but the daily work with the breed that brings a smile to my face. It is an acknowledgment that a dream has been fulfilled.

I have seen many breeds of horses walk into my training barn. Each one is different, and each one is talented. Drawing the analogy to people isn't difficult. Personalities, opportunities, and individual strengths and weaknesses are evident, making these horses all special. The trick is in communicating with them in a language they understand. Without appearing too bold, I can honestly say that, in forty years, I have never had a horse try to pitch me off that I have trained. That is not to say it couldn't happen. We all know horses can make liars out of us. However, I truly believe that if you do your homework with the animal and get it to focus and trust, then their fear of the unknown is dissipated in those first virgin rides.

Equine husbandry has also been a keen interest of mine. I have researched, enrolled in courses, and attended equine veterinary conferences as a guest. I have also produced and presented many professional health care workshops for the layperson over the years. This pivotal point in the wellbeing of the horse is constantly changing with new research and treatments. Staying abreast of important findings and other issues makes all of us better informed horse owners. It is true that horses are now outliving their teeth, making the statement "long in the tooth" all that more relevant.

Over the years, I became totally immersed in the equine phenomenon as my thirst for this passion intensified. I read, wrote, and published many articles on horses, which I continue to do today. One of my very earliest works was published in a Toronto magazine called *Bit and Bridle* when I was just thirteen or fourteen. The article was about the plight of the Caspian pony in Iran. I researched it on my own, corresponding with an American, Louise Firouz, who was living in Iran at the time. She was responsible for trying to save this ancient breed from extinction and was working with the king of Iran to establish a breeding program. Her story inspired me to write the tale and help bring awareness to the Caspian's potential untimely demise should their numbers continue to dwindle. A copy of the magazine with my article found its way into the royal stables in Iran and finally in the hands of the shah himself. I still have the letter I received from Tehran expressing the king's gratitude for helping bring awareness of the Caspian pony to the rest of the world. It may not have been a Pulitzer piece, but it sure made me feel like it. In the end, the Caspian pony survived the turmoil of the Iranian Revolution and can be found in sufficient numbers throughout the world. Although my contribution may seem small, I'm glad I was a part of this early rescue from extinction, if only by my words.

The people I have met, the students I have taught, the horses I have trained, and the goals they have achieved can only be measured in a contented heart. Seeing the joy etched on a rider's face that finally got the rhythm of the rising trot is reward in itself. Feeling a horse take those first few unsteady steps with someone on its back and then

Prologue

Impatiently, she squirms on the hot, sticky vinyl seat that pinches her young, slender thighs. The warm summer breeze fans her small face with temporary relief. She rolls the window crank down, a primitive source of air conditioning for vehicles of the '50s vintage. She imagines riding in a golden chariot like Cinderella as the horses beneath the hood of the old Ford station wagon carry her off to a magical place. She twirls her short, black curls that crown her head as she stares with boredom at the passing views.

As the miles and minutes pass, she entertains herself with visions of horses galloping across emerald fields dotted with bright yellow dandelions and buttercups. Rounding a bend in the road, she is momentarily shaken from her daydreams as a solemn horse grazes in a pasture close to the road. She pleads relentlessly with her father to stop the car. Reluctantly, he yields to her pleading calls. He slows the car as it crackles and crunches its way over the loose gravel onto the shoulder of the road. The car slowly rolls to a quiet, calculated stop. The little girl flings the door ajar and bounds out of the car.

As not to frighten the horse, she quickly slows her haste, quietly approaching the cedar rail fence. Her eyes dance with excitement, and her heart quickens its pace in response. She grabs a twist of long, lush, sweet grass and offers it to the curious horse with her hand outstretched in a gesture of good faith. The paint raises its head and cautiously sniffs the air for identification of friend or foe. Satisfied that the visitor is harmless, the horse approaches the tall, slender girl holding the token gift in her smallish grasp.

That little girl so long ago still shivers with excitement at the *clip-clop* sound of horses' hooves that are no longer imagined, but real. It has been a lifelong journey that I have sustained, never relinquishing the dream but rather nurturing it and keeping focused. My father, a dreamer himself, once told me, "Never stop dreaming. If you try long and hard enough to follow that dream, it will come true." His faith in a dream was tested many times during his life, and so it would be in mine. Still, our kindred spirits made us keepers of dreams, and as believers, our determination to follow the wave of passion rewards us with ultimate and fulfilling destinies.

My earliest memories of my introduction to the horse world were complements of my grandfather, who emigrated from England to Canada in the early 1900s. He was my horse connection and the one from whom I seemed to inherit this burning passion for horses.

I was but two years of age, sitting on Grandfather Payne's lap in the screened porch of his tiny, neat bungalow. We sipped hand-squeezed lemonade while the butterflies that floated through the air on bright orange and black silk wings entertained us. The English garden below burst with colour, and nature's sweet fragrance attracted the honeybees. Fairylike hummingbirds hovered over the flower petals, siphoning the sweet nectar through their needlepoint beaks. The sleepy afternoons were like a long summer drawl. I hung on his every word as my eyes looked upward into his strong, blue eyes. He was a fabulous storyteller. I remember him with his pipe cradled in the corner of his mouth. The grey smoke rose in the hot midday air. The pipe would slip slowly from his lips only when his thoughts were gathered sufficiently to reminiscence for a while about his wonderful horses.

There was Babe and Teddy, the dairy horses that were his partners when he worked at City Dairy in Toronto. Later, the Massey family-owned company amalgamated with Borden Dairy and fell under its corporate umbrella. It was during the lean Depression years when my grandfather's weekly wage was twenty-five dollars earned over a twelve to thirteen-hour day, seven days a week, with only the occasional day off. You could count on one hand the number of days off Grandfather took during his long tenure as an employee of the dairy. It was considered a rather good wage for those times, and the dairy was extremely kind to its employees, according to my mother. That twenty-five dollars was frugally divvied up to cover the rent on the house, as well as to feed and clothe a family of five. There really wasn't much left over to enjoy the social things in life or entertain three young children. Still, it was work, and he was glad to be employed.

In winter, it was the care of his four-legged comrades, the horses, which made his rise from a warm bed at just after midnight a must. He would dash out to catch the last streetcar at the first hour of the morning as he headed off to the dairy to feed and prepare his horse. The soft sideways mashing of hay created by the horse's mandibles as it pulverized the succulent blades of timothy and brome grasses between its teeth was rewarded with utter contentment. The rhythmic sound of horses at feed soothed any worries of the day ahead and lightened one's soul. The stable was bathed in peaceful serenity. Life could be simple as Grandfather cheerfully whistled his favourite tune, "The Missouri Waltz." After he forked the last shafts of dried hay into the rough wooden manger, he continued to whistle his way along the red brick floor and out of the stable. Totally awakened with the freshness of the day, he briskly walked the brief city blocks to the dairy.

There was a checklist of things to be done before the wheels of the heavily laden milk wagon began to roll out of the cobblestone yard. With the freezing chill of winter, dairy products needed to be delivered and retrieved from the customers' milk boxes before the plummeting temperatures froze the bottles solid. In summer, the start to the day's routine was delayed by several hours, granting a few more hours of precious sleep. Still, the dairy products had to reach the consumer before the heat of noon spoiled the sensitive goods.

Grandfather prepared his horse's midday feedbag for the road and loaded his wagon with milk, butter, cheese, eggs, and cream. With his wagon stash of farm-fresh dairy products, his daily route led him through the sleepy streets of Toronto. He would travel into the early dawn and hustle of morning travellers on their way to work. Since refrigeration was a problem during those days, early delivery before the heat of the day crept in was necessary. A spoiled bottle of milk was not acceptable. By 11:15 a.m., the horses were led to the communal water trough at the corner of Queen and Yonge streets. The checks holding their head up while in harness were released allowing the horses to stretch their necks. They could then drink freely without the tether effect of the check rein. The horses stretched long and low to sip the refreshing, cool water. With their thirst quenched, Grandfather retrieved the feedbag loaded with fresh oats to rejuvenate their depleted energy stores. The horses were left tied to a hitching post while Grandfather stole away for a quick bite of a savoury roast beef sandwich served on freshly baked bread from a hot wood oven. The hungry man meal was washed down with a pint of buttermilk retrieved from an ice-filled crate in the back of the wagon.

He would arrive back at the dairy yard in early afternoon, tired and relieved. He dropped the check from the harness, letting the horse lower its nose from the restraint. Grandfather began to undo the tight wraps and remove the traces from the whiffletree[1]. The heavy collar hugged by the steel hames was lathered with hard work and rank with horse sweat. The collar was twisted upside down and slipped over the horse's weary head. Released from the bonds of the cumbersome wagon and led into the stable, the horse enjoyed the

---

1   A Whippletree is a loose, horizontal bar that the traces or long leather straps of the harness attach to. The bar is connected to the wagon or load and distributes the load more evenly.

bristle of the dandy brush over its broad back and down its feathered legs. Grandfather continued to massage the horse's fatigued muscles for several minutes. He tossed and fluffed fresh straw, taking special care to bank the walls and corners of the roomy standing stall. At last, he placed several flakes of hay in the manger and poured quarts of grain into the corner feeder. The harness was wiped and hung in its designated place. Grandfather gathered up the empties from the day and met the cashier, handing over his tickets and cash sales from his route. Back out on the street, he waited patiently. He sighed with a deep breath while straining to hear the clang of the streetcar coming to carry him home. The horse could retire for the remainder of the day until the clock on the mantel struck midnight, and the process began again.

Through these early horse tales, I learned at a young age how personable, intelligent, and courageous the horse can be. We just need to take the time to listen and observe the horse language. If you cup your ear with your hand and tilt your head very carefully, you can hear imagined calk-shod hooves tap dancing on the brick and cobblestone surface of the high society streets of Toronto.

Every day with regularity, Teddy jogged by the stately manors nestled among the princely gardens known as Rosedale. The wagon jostled its way along as he pushed into his collar and approached the notoriously steep incline at Hog's Hollow. Grandfather broke into a tender smile as he told of Teddy's clever technique of managing the long walk down into the valley when the roads became treacherous and slick underfoot. The stout, dapple grey Percheron gelding would position himself at the crest of the hill and drop to his haunches. He basically sat on his tail and put his front legs out in front to act as brakes. From the top of the hill, Teddy slid cautiously down the hill, bringing the wagon to a halt by digging in his heels. The borium studs on his shoes trailed a grooved path in the glassy ice and snow. Finally, his shoes took firm hold. He stood up and nonchalantly continued his route.

Like his predecessor, the black mare named Babe, Teddy often drove home to the dairy with a sleep-deprived whip (driver) holding the lines. Whether it was the position of the traffic light or the movement of notorious stink wagons that rattled along the streets and polluted the sweet country air, Teddy knew when to halt and wait for the lights to change. Teddy and Babe would bring Grandfather home safely to the dairy courtyard day after day. More than once, a neighbour would spot Grandfather asleep with his dreams while the horse patiently waited for the light to change. The horse would push into his collar and walk with the flow of traffic.

The horses had their favourite customers, too. As Grandfather told it, Babe wouldn't budge from one stop on the route until the lady of the house came out with a lump of sugar. Once the mare crunched down on the tasty treat, Babe would engage her hindquarters and walk off. Getting Babe to move from her benefactor's yard if her sugar gift was not presented to her would be a challenge. Grandfather scolded her with a sharp tongue-lashing while begging her to "walk on." With great reluctance, Babe would drop her downcast head and proceed begrudgingly as if swearing under her breath.

With the last puff of his pipe, Grandfather set it down as he took my hand and gently lowered me to the floor. "Let's go see the Gee Gee," he announced upon the arrival of the bread wagon. Off we went, the screen door slapping its approval behind us. I skipped along the path, firmly clasping Grandfather's strong hand, secure in the knowledge that the horses knew him. The carthorse raised his bored and weary head as we approached. Grandfather took my hand, instructing me to uncurl my fingers as he placed a hard rock of sugar on my flattened palm. The horse perked its ears forward and telescoped its neck to reach the bite-sized treat. I remember its whiskers tickling my hand as it blew softly against my skin before snatching away the sugar. I looked in amazement at its enormous hooves while being very conscious of my own tiny toes. I can still hear the wheels of Silverwood's white wagon rolling along the pavement following that methodical *clip-clop* of the horse's shoes so long ago.

Grandfather and milk wagon

My last recollection of Grandfather is of him waving a sad goodbye as he peered out of his hospital window. Children weren't allowed to visit, and so I stole my last farewell from afar. I strained to catch a glimpse of Grandfather waving from his hospital window high atop. Grandfather had become a victim of his pipe, which was his favourite pastime. His fragile lungs, tortured by the mustard gas that clouded the slick trenches of World War I, could not survive another attack. Lung cancer would claim another casualty and deprive me of my loving Grandfather. How I cursed that addiction and promised myself I wouldn't touch the deadly weed and I never have.

Chapter 1

The Flood Pant Years

It would be a number of years before I was able to resume my pastime with horses. Dressed in too-short pants we often referred to as "flood pants," my childhood was perfect as childhoods go. We lived in the north country of Ontario on the outskirts of North Bay, not far from the rocky shores of Trout Lake. School buses weren't available to us, so I rode my bicycle to school on late spring days. During the long winter months when the temperature dropped to minus twenty-three degrees Celsius or lower, I hitched a ride in the back of an old pickup with rust-devoured fenders that flapped spontaneously in the icy wind. My companions and I huddled behind the centre wall of the cab. It sheltered us from the frostbiting wind of an absent old Keewadin.[2] On other occasions, we bundled up in our wool winter coats and put on a pair of galoshes with the binding buckles that often froze and jammed with the snow. When the rubber seals of our boots began to leak, out would come plastic bags that we wrapped our feet in before putting on the Arctic wear. I don't think duct tape had been invented yet. Otherwise we all would have sported the familiar silvery grey tape design on our snow boots.

---

2   Keewadin is the Cree word meaning north-west wind that brings winter to the prairies.

The wintertime was particularly hard. Often I would make it home from school only to feel the painful sting of my toes and fingers as the warmth of the house started to thaw my frozen appendages. My dad would rub snow on our hands and feet in an attempt to lessen the sharp tingle of pain from thawing. The woolen mittens lay over the floor heat registers as the faint smell of sheep permeated the air. The mittens were left to dry for another day.

On one occasion, we were let out of school early because of a blinding snowstorm, only to be paralysed with the cold. I had a broken arm as a result of falling on ice, and I sported a sling and white autographed cast at the time. My schoolmate and neighbour, Bruce Knight, kept reassuring his seven-year-old friend that he would get us some help and that everything would be okay. My aboriginal friend became my saviour. He comforted me with his words of reassurance as we ploughed our way through waist-deep snowdrifts. He gently hugged my shoulders with soothing affection and steadied my one good arm as we tripped through the deepening snow. Quietly, he whispered, "Please don't cry. It will be all right." So I didn't cry.

Taking one step at a time in the now hip-high drifts of snow that swirled around us, we dredged our way to a little frame house only barely visible through the driving veil of snow. An older couple greeted us at the door and quickly whisked us into their warm home. I remember the kind lady helping me take off my stiff and frozen wool coat. She was horrified to find that the sleeve of my coat had been hiding a white cast on my arm. It was scribbled with scrawl of juvenile penmanship. Her husband asked us for our names and home phone numbers while holding the receiver in one hand. Waiting in the comfort and security of their kitchen, we were treated to steamy hot chocolate with cream floating on top. A plate of freshly baked cookies was placed on the table as the rotary dial phone clicked away the numbers. Our worried parents were summoned, and once the snowplough had managed to clear enough passage, we arrived safely at our respective front doors within the hour.

Being raised in the gateway of the north, my childhood pals were mostly of French-Canadian, Italian, or Aboriginal descent. My closest companions while growing up were Aboriginals and Metis.[3]

We were true friends, relying on each other for protection and entertainment. Our playground was the secret forest and happy meadows. Our landscape was not of concrete and brick but of wildflowers, strawberries, rocky blueberries patches, and fields of raspberry canes. We rode our handmade stick horses through the bracken ferns and rocks, practicing our horsemanship on our make-believe mounts. Occasionally, the snakes that lived beneath the fallen trees and rock crevices would startle us. Garter snakes were a common sight, along with an assortment of wildlife from snapping turtles and crabs in the creek to spiny porcupines, rabbits, skunks, and even a mother black bear and her cubs. I never walked in the creek without wearing sandals, as I feared the crabs would bite my toes or a fish would nibble away at my foot. But mostly I feared the snakes.

One day, while kicking rocks along the dusty dirt road following our small troupe of cavaliers, we came upon a very large snake. It was coiled and ready to strike as it lay in the middle of the road. It could have been a massasauga rattlesnake, but I wasn't sure. None of us could pass safely by this silent predator, so only one person was allowed to circle by very slowly. Our guardian at the time, Joe Knight sent her eldest boy to fetch the axe resting against the wall of their house by the back screen door. I can tell you that she could wield an axe with deadly accuracy. That snake never knew what hit it.

Down the road from us lived the retired draft horse that was appropriately named Chubby. I would often visit Chubby, taking him an apple from my threadbare back pocket. I had rubbed and polished it with vigour on my right pant leg, buffing the fruit to a bright, ruby red hue. Chubby's big, lumbering body would slowly

---

3   The Metis are recognized as Aboriginal peoples of Canada. They are descendents of Native Indian and European or French-Canadian marriages.

make its way to me when I appeared at the fence. Standing on the bottom rail and hanging my arms over the rough post of the top rail, I called to him.

Chubby disliked snakes. If you tiptoed through his pasture in late summer, you would find the remnants of these reptiles that were left squished in the field. I once witnessed Chubby defending his grazing lands from these ground crawlers. He stood on his hind legs and pulverized the snake into the ground with his dinner-plate-sized front feet. Again and again, he reared and fell until the snake lay still. A ton of horseflesh could flatten anything beyond recognition. Chubby was a master of snake control. You might say he was the St. Patty of the horse world, driving the snakes away from his sacred pasture.

One day, I went to visit my friendly chestnut gelding. His pasture was empty and eerily silent. I asked Mr Farmer (no pun intended; that was his real name) where Chubby was. He merely replied that he went away. I guess it was his subtle way of telling me that Chubby had gone to greener pastures. Still, I missed my daily visits with this kind old horse that had been my first constant connection to horses. I would soon have to find another horse that I could latch on to. Losing Chubby and finding a whole stable of horses was a turning point in my young life that would prove to be the catalyst in my lifelong horse adventure.

Even with Chubby gone, I still made regular visits to his pasture and his owners. They had a beautiful garden of flowers. Mr Farmer often invited me to stroll through the maze of colour as he snipped some of his rainbow beauties from his garden patch and handed them to me from his dry, rough farmer hands. "Give these to your mother," he responded with a crooked smile. With my hands barely containing the mountain of fresh-cut flowers, his wife would swing the screen door open and invite me in. The whiff of fresh-baked cookies was an irresistible treat. These kindly folks were not forgotten in my nightly prayers.

For the next few years, I had to be content riding the mechanical horse at the local grocery store. As I tugged at my mother's sleeve and pleaded anxiously with my parents to be allowed to ride the whimsical horse, they relented by dropping a dime into the slot. The horse started rolling along, mimicking some semblance of the canter without variance of speed or cadence. Still, I could dream about riding a real horse as I rocked forward and back to the rhythm of the pretend horse beneath me.

It was the spring of 1962 when I first discovered that there was a stable fairly close by. I could make it on my bicycle in good weather. After fall freeze-up, I found a shortcut. Following a crude, snow-packed deer path through the swamp, I could get to the road leading to the stable. It wasn't the sort of path you took when nightfall came. The wolf and lynx became the chosen predators of the swamp as darkness fell.

I started hanging around the stable that first spring. I offered to help the old man who lived on the premises and looked after the horses from morning to night. The stable housed a small herd of ponies and Standardbred horses, along with a few boarded saddle horses. A fellow who operated the local drive-in theatre owned the property. Adjacent to the drive-in theatre was the stable with its distinct odour that only horse lovers appreciated.

Every Saturday night, pony rides were offered for twenty-five cents. I soon had a job volunteering to lead the ponies in the paddock. School was out, and the summer evenings were long. Pony rides were a main attraction at the drive-in theatre. An endless line of Chevys, Fords, and Dodges carrying their passengers of weary moms and bored dads shouting their complaints to their hollering and excited children drove around at turtle speed looking for an ideal vantage point. Young lovers seeking the sanctuary of a passion pit on wheels paraded in an orderly fashion through the ticket gate, only to be lost in the secluded back row. The sweet sound of Andy Williams belting out the hit song "Moon River" pumped through silvery grey speaker mounts. With the windows cranked down and the heavy metal speakers resting against the glass of the car door window, a match lit the mosquito coil on the dash. Presto! The family was settled and ready for show time.

I walked the ponies in endless circles until the sun began to lose its strength, and the projection screen came to life. Once in a while, I would stay a little longer to catch tidbits of a movie from the grassy knoll of the stable. The buttery smell of fresh popping corn drifted in the night air, tempting me to stroll to the concession booth. With only pennies in my pocket, alas, my taste buds would have to wait. As the light of day bequeathed itself to nightfall, I pedalled my bicycle home.

During the weekdays, the outside lane of the theatre doubled as a training track for the Standardbreds. I often got to hot walk the racehorses after their workouts when school was out for the summer. One day, I was handed the lines of an old racehorse named Morning Glory. I think my heart stopped. At fifteen, Glory was still racing on the *B* tracks. He was a relic by racing standards when most careers are well over by age five or six. Glory was one of my favourite boys. I was only supposed to jog the horse down and start cooling him off as I swung my skinny leg over the heel of the jogger and settled into the not-so-forgiving seat.

Glory had other ideas. He quickly got on gait, and I felt we were flying. I just kept him on the track, figuring he would eventually wear down. The speaker poles whizzed by. It was quite thrilling, actually, although I think I had a white-knuckle grip on the lines. Glory and I became fast friends, and I always cheered for him when he raced at the local track, Sunnydale Racetrack. I memorized his pole and saddlecloth number before the race so that I could watch for him in the pack as they made their dash to the wire. He was a champion in my eyes even if he only won the occasional race. I got to walk him back to the racetrack shedrow[4] after the race, taking a wide margin as we passed the open stall door of the favourite money winner, Nipper. I can assure you that the horse lived up to his name. It seems that the more aggressive the temperament, the tougher the competitor. Still, I had a soft spot for old Glory.

I also had another favourite racehorse at the stable. He was the mysterious stallion kept segregated from the rest of the stable where he stood alone in his dropped ceiling but roomy box. His name was Claude Hanover, a product of the famous breeding and racing stable Hanover Shoe Farms from Hanover, Pennsylvania. Jean Burrows of North Bay owned the classy stallion for many years. Jean, a large-boned woman with a strong character and mannerisms to match, often accompanied her elderly father to the stable. Mr Burrows, on the other hand, was a dapper man of quiet dignity and social graces. I remember being impressed by his spritely step and friendly manner. He made it a point to come over to speak with me, always calling me by my first name. It made me feel important.

Claude Hanover was foaled in 1949, a son of Nibble Hanover out of the mare Amy Jane by Highland Scott. His career earnings were modestly successful for his era, banking $31,000 and change. He sired twenty-nine offspring. As a broodmare sire, he produced thirteen dams that in turn produced sixty-five foals. Their purses totalled almost $800,000. His best offspring was Moorelands Jean, a trotter who earned over $36,000 in her racing career during the late 1960s and early seventies.

Claude Hanover was a handsome and intelligent bay horse. In those days, girls weren't allowed to handle stallions or even enter the stall. Stallions were totally off limits. I had to admire Claude from the bars on his stall that separated us. He had a curious habit of flipping the air with his lower lip, which was surely a boredom thing. It wasn't cribbing, but it was an oddity I have never seen again.

---

4   A long line of horse stalls at a racetrack.

I don't think he had a mean bone in his body and was always the gentleman. Claude Hanover was my positive introduction to stallions and an image that would serve me well in later years. Even when they led him out of his stall for playtime in the sand paddock, he walked with quiet nobility.

I was given the responsibility of grooming and handling numerous ponies at the stable. One of the most cantankerous fellows was a dark bay/Hackney cross named Barney. You always had to watch yourself when putting the grain in his bin. Barney was known as a "crowder," and one day, I found out why the term was so fitting. Actually, I would have more aptly described him as a "crusher."

The gospel, according to management, was that those of us who volunteered at the farm were to always be aware and to let the horses know that you were there. Safety rules were drilled into us. Any infractions of these rules meant an automatic ban from the barn with no return. We all took the rules of the stable seriously. Barney was a sly devil that delighted in always having the upper hand. As I approached him from behind, coming between him and the wall, Barney made his move. He pinned me with his left hip against the wall. He squeezed so hard that I couldn't breathe. I remember starting to black out as I wiggled seemingly for an eternity, trying to free myself of his crushing weight. Panic-stricken, I somehow squirmed my way toward his shoulders and head, gasping for air all the way. I made a rather hasty exit from the stall using the far side. I never entered his stall again without the protection of a pitchfork in hand to ward off his advances. Needless to say, Barney knew his game was up and never attempted to wrestle with me again.

Barney hadn't finished taunting me. A bad penny, his unsavoury stable manners extended to outdoor activities, as well. He was just as ornery and malicious under saddle. He played great delight in dropping to his knees while trying to roll people off his back. The first time it happened to me, I was dumbfounded. He crashed to the ground in seconds. Barney had been trotting around the paddock, his gait typically short and choppy, when all of a sudden, he hit the dirt and rolled over on me. I could hardly move my leg after he had mangled it into the heavy sand gravel of the paddock. I was certain he had crushed it. I remember limping home and hiding my pain from my parents. I feared that if they knew what had happened, I might never see the stable again. Luckily, my leg was just badly bruised, causing me grief for a week or more. You learn tolerance of pain quickly if you think an overly protective parent who just doesn't understand your passion to be with horses could jeopardize your visits to the stable. You suffer in silence.

The next time I rode the devil mule Barney, I was more than adequately prepared for his antics. I hadn't been long in the saddle when I could detect that he was starting to gather himself up. This time, I was ready with a hefty whip and determined to use it at all costs. When he started to buckle beneath me, I gave him one tremendous slap with the crop, using all of my strength. I think the adrenaline had kicked in, as well, making it a double-hard sting of the crop. Feeling the sharp, searing sting from the stick, Barney bolted back up, pinned his sullen ears, and walked on without any more nonsense. The best thing that could be said about Barney was that he made me conscious of my surroundings and his deceptive pranks. I never became complacent and learned to analyze and respond quickly. If you weren't heeding his subtle warnings, you were fair game. He preyed on the novices, laughing, I'm certain, every time he succeeded at one of his well-executed tactical deployments.

We had many other ponies that were a delight to ride and who were patient teachers. In my opinion, ponies tend to get a bad rap most of the time. People often forget that ponies are nothing more than small horses and should be considered as such. Too often, they get labelled as tyrants and untrustworthy mounts. That may have been true in the case of Barney, but he was the exception rather than the rule. The blame lies more with the inexperienced rider who torments the pony with uneducated hands that yank and pull on the bars in the pony's tender mouth. Riders with active, impatient legs deliver hard, unwarranted kicks to pony's sides as punishment. Sulking children take out their inadequacies and frustrations on the pony by pounding on their backs and yelling in their ears. In praise of ponies, I think they are more like saints for what they are willing to endure. When they do act out, it most likely is for their own survival. Put a few inches on them and they become horses again that more mature, experienced adults can ride. The problem soon goes away as the size and intellect of the rider and pony are matched.

One of the smartest ponies at the stable was a brown and white pinto Shetland named Teddy. Teddy had a funny step to his gait. When he walked, the right hind leg would twist and rotate abruptly with each step. Despite this oddity, Teddy rode well and drove in harness. He learned a number of circus tricks along the way and was quite entertaining. Teddy was the pony we all had the most fun with. He demonstrated extreme patience with his young riders. Teddy's bag of tricks included bowing, placing all four feet on a small pedestal, and ground tying. Ground tying involves dropping a lead or rein that is attached to the horse's halter or bridle and letting it fall to the ground. Once the lead or rein makes contact with the ground, the horse is trained to stand without moving. Teddy would patiently stand where placed for more than an hour at a time. He was one smart cookie.

There were others that also came along and joined the swelling pony herd. One of these newcomers was Sailor, the grey pony of diminutive size with the silver mane and tail. He lacked confidence, but still was a treasure and delight despite his timid nature. There was a special little red chestnut mare named Cherry. She had been bred to an Arabian stallion and was in foal when she arrived at the stable.

One Saturday close to Easter, I pedalled into the yard and propped my bicycle against the side of the blue-painted building. I opened the one-man gate that allowed entry into the paddock and stable entrance. I clicked the latch shut and lazily sauntered into the stable. When I arrived in the barn, I was summoned to the tiny tack shop at the back of the stable. The distinct aroma of newly tanned leather that permeated the room and shiny new bits of steel that hung on the wall teased my senses and invited me in. The proprietor of the stable, a round little Italian man by the name of Romeo Veltri, had been quietly keeping watch over my barn duties. I remember him smiling at me as he sat on his proper chair at the end of a long, formidable desk. Still in repose, he pulled a bag from behind his squat body and presented me with a gift. "Happy Easter," he said with a mischievous wink. "I'm giving you an Easter bonnet." My eyes widened as I peered into the nondescript, brown paper bag and pulled out a black velvet riding helmet. I'd never seen such a beautiful thing and quickly popped it on my head for sizing. Helmets were treated more as a status symbol back then, as only the more wealthy people could afford them. They weren't the fashion, especially in a Western riding community like the environment I found myself living in. Still, I was so proud of that hat. He must have been chuckling inside as he said, "I think you need something to go with the helmet." He strode over to the back of the store, bending over with a groan, and brought out a brand-new pony English saddle and bridle. It was even better than Christmas! I was speechless in my shyness, but I think it was quite evident from the expression on my face that I was excited. I remember thanking him with good graces, but, shy as I was, I didn't want to appear too grateful. I don't know how many times I said "thank you" in my head. The tack would be a loaner for a pony I would be given full charge of for as long as I wanted. The deal was that I must work hard around the stable to enjoy the privilege of riding the pony of my choice, Cherry. There was no doubt that I would bond with this pony and complete my part of the bargain for the remainder of my childhood days in the north. You couldn't pry me away from the stable.

My home life seemed rather ho-hum in comparison to life at the barn. My older brother often teased me, nicknaming me Stinky. It didn't bother me. I liked the smell of horse even if I was called Stinky. I felt really honoured to be allowed to ride a pony. It was something other little girls only dreamed about, and I had fantasized about it for so long. Like most young children, my room wasn't as clean or tidy as the pony's stall. My mother often complained to me, "Why can't you keep your room as well as you look after that pony?" I had no excuse. The pony just seemed more important to me than my room, and I was like the second mother-in-waiting as the pony ballooned in size as her foaling date approached.

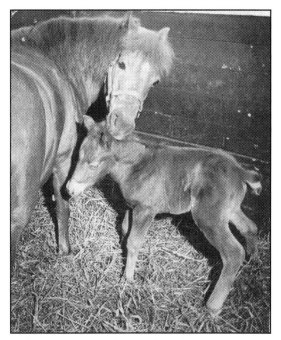

Cherry and foal

My father was a self-employed inventor, fixing television sets in the basement of our home while working on his long-distance television transmission inventions. My mother was a homemaker and looked after the family. She was a constant stabilizer in our lives. Money was always in short supply, so my horse habit was not supplemented in any way. I was financially strapped, a common complaint and disease of horse owners. What I learned about horses was what I observed or read up until this time. I never had the luxury of riding lessons during my life in the north, so I was basically self-taught during these early years. Once a month after church, I would stop at a local smoke shop where they carried the magazine *Western Horseman*. I saved my allowance so that I could purchase this horse digest. I read it from cover to cover while sitting cross-legged on my bed. The light on my nightstand burned well into the late evening. Books would be my tutors, but I was also very fortunate to have the wise old stable hand educate me in the real world of horses.

Chapter 2

A Mentor

Elzier Pigeau, center

Elzier Pigeau was the elderly fellow who lived on the premises and cared for the horses. He was a confirmed bachelor, either by design or misfortune. I never knew much about his past except that he was alone with no family at the point in his life when I entered his world. I think what made him most endearing was his brilliant smile and gentle hugs of welcome despite his shy, reserved manner. He was a man of good grooming and cleanliness. There was never a bootlace undone or a shirt unbuttoned, and he always had a clean-shaven face. A small man in build but a giant in heart, Elzier Pigeau walked taller than his physical frame. His soothing voice, sometimes in French or maybe in English, calmed a nervous or fractious horse. I was acutely perceptive of his gentle way with horses; it was something I would aspire to emulate in later life. It was a gift he had that was truly inspiring. Horses would relax in his presence and quietly follow his lead. He taught me how to think like a horse and not like a human. We, as humans, complicate things. We analyze, strategize, and generally miss the very basics. A horse, on the other hand, thinks and acts quickly in simple, direct language. There is no blurring of lines in judgment or instruction.

Mr Pigeau encouraged me to dig deep into emotion and not be afraid to express it to the horse. A horse feeds off emotion, both in a person's voice and in subtle physical changes. If you look with a soft eye and feel with a soft heart, a horse will relax. If you speak tough and stand tough, you have its attention. Act indecisively and they won't trust or respect you. For a young, shy girl not yet in her teens and embarrassed by thoughts of failure in the eyes of others, this was a challenge of epic proportions. Awakening a still budding depth of soul I hadn't yet discovered would be difficult. I would succeed and find this connection with the horse that no one could dissolve. It spurred me on to learn more and more.

Elzier Pigeau taught me the value of believing in myself first. Only then can you truly become a partner with your horse. Every day was a new lesson that brought me closer to the old man as a teacher and mentor. I had found my grandfather again in Elzier Pigeau. My journey with horses would resume with more vigour and meaning, setting the stage for a lifelong commitment to horses.

His day began as the sun rose in the east with the dew still beaded on the perennial grass. He said goodnight behind a curtain of soft red sky as he wearily retired to the comfort of his bed. These days were repeated with regularity and unbroken routine. His apartment was attached to the long, oblong stable at the opposite end of the tack shop. It was by all accounts convenient. He just opened his door and entered the worn, plank flooring of the stable that creaked and groaned with every step.

Mr Pigeau never needed the benefit of an alarm clock to awaken him as long as Ginger was around. Ginger, the red chestnut gelding bearing Morgan blood in his parentage, lived in the first box stall. He would knock on the wall with his hoof precisely at 6:00 a.m. every morning. It was breakfast time, and he wouldn't stop pawing the wall until the radio sitting on the shelf outside his stall door was turned on. This signalled grain time. Ginger was the doer for the stable, never letting Mr Pigeau sleep in a few sacred moments more, not even on Christmas.

Mr Pigeau, as I knew him and acknowledged him out of respect, was one of the kindest human beings I would ever have the privilege of meeting. If we accomplish nothing more in our short lives than being a mentor to someone else, we will have made a profound impact on that individual's life. It would be Mr Pigeau's legacy to have helped me along the way in understanding the equine mentality and the endurance of the human spirit.

I adored the old gentleman who often spent his free time sharing his experiences in the wilderness logging camps of northern Quebec. Flipping the pages of his tired, faded photo album brought to life these adventures of life in the harsh bush. Like my grandfather, Mr Pigeau was a storyteller who entertained his captive audiences with tales of lore and yesteryear. I studied well under his tutelage. His patience, humour, and love of the horse would be the virtues I honoured him the most for. It would be a friendship that would last until his final days on this good earth. To him, I was always "Caddy." In broken English, we somehow found a way of communicating even if he couldn't pronounce my name correctly.

Once a year, a couple of us self-declared cleaning maids would have Mr Pigeau leave while we gave his apartment a sprucing up. He would humour us by going shopping for a couple of hours, leaving us to practice our somewhat lacking domestic skills. It wasn't much of a job for us, as he was immaculate, both in his housekeeping duties and in personal hygiene. For a bachelor, he kept a home better than most homemakers, and he could scurry up a delicious meal at the drop of a hat.

One day, we acquired an orphan foal, and I was selected to help Mr Pigeau nurse this baby to adulthood. He instructed me on how to start the foal on the bottle and how to mix the special life-giving formula. As the foal matured, we switched to having it drink from a pail. When my pony delivered her foal, I was already well versed in foal care. However, I wasn't prepared for Cherry's protective instincts concerning her newborn. I had been so involved with pampering the foal that Cherry finally had had enough. I had been neglecting her, and she let me know it with a nasty bite to my arm as if to say, "Leave the kid alone." The bruising left its imprint of purple and red teeth marks. From that day forward, I ensured equal attention for both her and her foal, hoping to diminish her jealousy.

As the years passed and our lives moved on, Mr Pigeau was always in my thoughts. For the moment, I will step into the future to reminisce about this very special person that remains to this day my mentor. Although it had been several years since I'd left the north, I had continued to communicate with old Mr Pigeau. He would often write me letters in his arthritic, shaky handwriting. He used simple words, as his writing in English was limited. His letters always made me smile and were my link to the past.

My parents always liked Elzier, and so we invited him for a weekend away from the stable. Permission was granted for him to take leave, and he soon headed south on a bus for Toronto. We collected him from the bus depot and brought him home to

Pickering. Mr Pigeau had always wondered what the Royal Winter Fair was like, as he had only heard about it. In all of his seventy-five years, he had never had the opportunity to attend. We were going to give him that gift.

With an admission ticket in his gnarled, weathered hand, he entered the turnstile of the horse palace. His quiet, pale blue eyes danced with excitement like a boy at Christmas. He was in awe and utterly speechless. The only words that would slip off his tongue were "Oh, my." He watched the heavies in all their blindingly bright brass hames and patent leather collars parade around the ring. He marvelled at the high-stepping Hackneys as they pranced through their paces with the fine viceroy buggies rolling along behind them. He took it all in and memorized every detail. His visit was too short. I wanted him to stay with us forever, but I knew the horses needed him back in North Bay. He packed his grip and reluctantly waited on the platform at the bus terminal. His freshly laundered shirt reflected the silent dignity the old man felt. He had enjoyed his adventure in the big city as he gently kissed me farewell. Tears of joy and sadness converged and trickled down his cheeks as he waved *au revoir*. He was a sensitive man and unashamed to display his emotions and his love of friends.

A short time later, I received a letter from the stable in North Bay with some devastating news. Mr Pigeau had been diagnosed with bone cancer in his leg. The stubborn little Frenchman would not allow them to amputate his leg. He had signed his own death warrant with his decision. Still, I could understand how an elderly person who had lived a fairly healthy existence would want to leave this world intact. Who was I to argue any differently? The letter indicated that he was being treated in the hospital at Sturgeon Falls. I arranged to catch a bus to North Bay and then transfer to Sturgeon Falls. I would stay overnight in North Bay and then return the following day. With my little weekender in hand, I boarded the bus and began the four-hour ride to North Bay.

Bus rides always made me nauseous. Perhaps it was the constant groan of the diesel engine or its poisonous exhaust. Maybe it was the roll and pitch of the carriage. I never could ride a bus comfortably, and this long tour required strong mental control of my stomach, which was in turmoil. I managed to suppress the urge to vomit, finding relief by pressing my clammy face against the coolness of the window.

At North Bay, I transferred buses and headed off for the relatively short trip to Sturgeon Falls. I was the only passenger to be let off when we reached the small French-speaking community. There was no welcoming committee; there was just a shack of a hotel and bar on the corner. I was alone and a little apprehensive as I followed the sign indicating the hospital. I marched along the side of the road, never giving indication that I was at all afraid. I took a strong stride and held my head up. I learned long ago that if you appear bold, most animals will back off. I figured that people would probably respect a strong individual rather than a weakling. How else was this young woman of the world able to protect herself from predators and bullies? I certainly wasn't strong enough to fight off an attacker, so my ultimate plan was to appear uninhibited.

My journey to the hospital was uneventful other than the occasional stare from local inhabitants. My French was nonexistent, and no one spoke English or at least admitted to it. I asked for Mr Pigeau and was kindly directed to his ward. I entered the room where I found him dozing off, his pillow raised just enough so that he didn't lie totally prostrate on the bed. I called his name, and as if waking from a dream, his eyes opened, and he smiled broadly. "My dear Caddy!" he exclaimed to everyone in the room. He babbled away in French to his neighbours before signalling me to take up a chair. He complimented me on my blossoming maturity. We laughed and reminisced about our time together at the stable. Not once did either of us mention his cancer. It seemed taboo, and I had come to offer moral support, not to lecture a dying old man who obviously had made his peace with God. I was to be his only company in a long while. His family had long since passed away, and there were no close relatives to care for him. I stayed a few hours before the nurses came and gently told Elzier that I must go. He translated for me, and I kissed and hugged him one last time. I was crying inside as I walked back to the bus stop, this time in a crestfallen manner. I realized that I would never see the sweet old man again that had taught me so much. I prayed that his suffering wouldn't be too great. He deserved that much. Mr Pigeau died shortly after my visit, and I grieve for him still.

Chapter 3

Life's Lessons

There were a few sad times at the stable when I was growing up as a young girl. Tragedies happen despite our best efforts to guard against them. So was the story of Charlie, a three-year-old bay thoroughbred gelding and ex-racehorse turned pleasure horse that was boarded at the stable.

One cold winter's day, Charlie carried his young mistress out on the snow-covered road on a late afternoon hack. The brilliant sun illuminated the diamond white crystals of snow. They danced in the air, whirling in concert with the light bite of the north wind. Linda hadn't owned the horse for very long. She and her American family lived on the military base of the North American Aerospace Defence Command (NORAD). NORAD was built in the 1950s in response to the Cold War era that existed. The NORAD complex was a huge underground bunker positioned deep within the rocky hillside on the shores of Trout Lake. It was a secretive and secure facility sheltered and guarded from the public eye. The bi-national defence team's base was very close to our stables. The stables were an ideal location for Linda to board her horse in such close proximity to her home.

It was a get-acquainted period for both Linda and her horse starting with their short daily hacks. Danger hid beneath a light dusting of snow as Charlie lifted one bare hoof at a time, contacting the ground evenly and calculatingly, unaware of the treacherous footing below. In an instant, poor Charlie found himself prostrate on the ground a few yards from the stable. After several attempts at rising, he staggered helplessly to his feet. His hind legs had separated and spread sideways when the edge of his rear hoof slid away from his body on the ice. Charlie hobbled home. Lame and in pain, it must have been a pitiful sight to watch as Charlie struggled to drag his hind legs behind.

A veterinarian was summoned immediately. It was serious business, and the prognosis from Doc Smilie wasn't good. Still, an attempt was made to help heal Charlie's injured hind legs and make him as comfortable as possible. It would be a long convalescence with no guarantee of success. The veterinary college at the University of Guelph was some 250 miles away. Charlie was in no condition to make the trip without the benefit of his hind legs to support him. It was a quandary as to how best treat the horse. Finally, a hasty plan of action was put into place, and Charlie was confined to stall rest. It was a sort of wait-and-see tactic.

For weeks, Charlie's belly lay in a sling supported by a block and tackle hanging from the beams of the stable. He was hand fed and watered. It was a job we all took turns doing without complaint. Charlie didn't struggle. Despite his obvious suffering, he still pricked his ears forward when we offered him his hay and mash as he valiantly hid his pain from us. Weeks passed as we waited and held our breath to see if Charlie was going to recover.

We weren't allowed in the stable the day of Charlie's assessment. We only heard that when the sling was removed, Charlie could no longer support himself and repeated his earlier injury with even more devastating results. This time, a quick injection by a veterinarian's needle ended any prolonged suffering.

My faced drained and my stomach knotted when I received the news. I had never really known death before, human or animal, except for my grandfather's. I was the last one who fed and groomed poor Charlie, thinking I would see him standing on his own four feet that evening. How could it be that he was dead? He had struggled for so long and never once showed aggression in his confined, awkward state. It wasn't fair, I thought.

I lived, breathed, and dreamed horses. For once in my young life, I had the opportunity to be a part of the horse world, and it was fabulous. My life after school was filled with hours of grooming the ponies until their hides shone like a new copper penny. My summers meant trail rides in the forest. Just the gentle rock from side to side of the pony moving beneath me gave me a rush of ecstasy. It was great to be alive and partnered with my pony.

I recall one momentous ride in late summer, climbing up the meandering, crude road that led to the water reservoir. It was a rocky climb up the hill where it grew into a plateau, giving way to hundreds of more pine, maple, and broad oak trees. The occasional tree fell across our path. It was a natural obstacle with which we could practice our jumping techniques. There were three of us from the stable that rode out on Sailor, Teddy and Cherry. My companions were also young girls who volunteered at the stable. Our ponies were quick and agile as we flew over the downed trees on our imaginary winged Pegasus, that mythical flying horse. The hack made us warm. Beads of perspiration slowly trickled down our foreheads. We pulled up our ponies, letting them hang their heads. We slid our jackets off our shoulders and tied the arms carelessly around our slender waists. We laughed and chatted for a spell before surveying the woods and deciding it was time to move on. We legged up the ponies and travelled down the rough granite path. We were always on the lookout for those horrible snakes that occasionally slithered past us.

As we approached a large maple tree, the ponies stopped dead in their tracks. They nervously danced on the spot like well-trained dressage mounts executing a piaffe.[5] The ponies begged us to retreat, but instead we held them fast. We attempted to reassure them that it was only their imaginations and that there honestly wasn't anything there. We couldn't understand what all the fuss was about until we looked closer at the suspect tree. The claws of a bear marking ownership of its territory had scarred the bark. The tree's wounds were fresh enough that the bear's scent was still present!

Bears were common inhabitants of the area. We would often have to crouch down and pan a field of wild raspberry canes with our eyes before declaring the area a bear-free zone. The bears loved berries, too, and it wasn't a good idea to share the community wealth at the same time, especially if the bear had a cub or two at her side. You could always tell that the bears had beaten us to the patch. Besides the obvious signs of bear scat, the black devils seemed to delight in trampling the canes and flattening grassy sections of the meadow where they lay in peaceful bliss after consuming large bushel amounts of berries.

In order to trap or destroy troublesome bears, horsemeat was sometimes used to bait them. I'm certain our ponies would have been considered delicacies if a bear had gotten a whiff of them.

We heard a heavy rustling in the dense brush just ahead. We put two and two together. The ponies turned on their haunches quicker than any reining horse as they retreated down that rocky trail. We never looked back but charged ahead at racehorse speed. I don't really remember which one of us had the lead. It must have been a head-to-head scamper as none of us were close enough to eat each other's dust. I think I had a few bruises on my knee where I bumped the pony ahead of me in our dash to safety.

---

5   The piaffe is an energetic and highly collected and elevated trot with no forward movement. The horse remains trotting on the spot.

I was once ponied beside an average-sized horse while mounted on a giant Standardbred gelding named Jimmy. By the stick, he measured well over seventeen hands. My skinny, wiry frame got lost on his long back. This was a far cry from riding twelve to thirteen-hand ponies. A lead shank ran from his halter underneath the bridle to the hands of a dashing young Royal Canadian Mounted Police officer. The handsome officer was visiting the stable and was going out on a hack. He took a shine to me, I guess, and he invited me to join him. I was to get the "real feel" of a trot atop this Mount Everest of horses. As Jimmy began to trot the familiar diagonal and not the lateral pacing gate, the young officer on the normal-sized horse cantered to keep up with Jimmy's daddy longlegs reach. Jimmy's stride grew, and the drive off his hip was catapulting. Soon, the horse beside me was galloping alongside Jimmy's monstrous trot. The tethering line was my only security, and it was now being stretched against the strain. My hands gripped the reins in a response to slow the big guy down. It was my very first riding lesson, and what better than to have a gorgeous and talented officer teach me the finer points of equitation? Posting on Jimmy was difficult but necessary. Otherwise, I got left behind, and the thought of bailing off onto the road from that height forced me to pay attention and stay in rhythm. I didn't dare stop riding, as the consequences would be catastrophic. All I could hear was my instructor saying, "Keep with him!" as the pounding hooves grew louder and quicker.

I was always a little cautious around Jimmy even before my memorable ride. He had been struck by lightning, and the rumour had it that he was just a touch crazy. He bore the white telltale line of fried hide down his back where the shock had burned and scarred him. The big horse was friendly enough and calm most of the time. He would, however, become a little squirrelly on occasion. You just had to be aware and stay out of reach of his front hooves when he was feeling fresh. Jimmy was a lesson in self-preservation at the trot.

Chapter 4

Wagging Tails and Other Creatures

Besides a propensity toward horses, I loved the dogs in my life. Dogs and horses just seem to go together naturally. I had a rather bizarre collection of other animals and reptiles. Like most children, I brought home strays and orphans whether they were feline or canine. I also loved my turtles and had six at one time. I would lazily walk the path leading to the creek with a bucket and a small net in hand. I squatted precariously on a moist rock, spying intently into the water. A small school of pinheads wiggled their way to their ultimate doom. I swooped down with my net and scooped them up. My turtles would have a fish dinner tonight. I transferred the delectable pinheads from my minnow bucket to the turtle bowl. The tiny fish didn't last long. Turtles might be slow movers on land, but they are masters in the water and can strike like a flash. They can snatch up the quick minnows in the blink of an eye. Slowpoke was my favourite, and when he passed on, I put him in a small matchbox coffin and buried him high on the hill. Little plastic flowers marked his tiny grave that Good Friday in April. I made a final tearful farewell.

Toads were also big on my list of favourite amphibians. I collected baby toads and released them at night. They always intrigued me. It is funny that I never liked the feel of frogs and their slimy green skin. Toads were rugged and bigger, I guess, even if they did pee on me. The myth was that if a toad peed on you, you would get warts. It never happened.

At night, my brother and I bottled fireflies and marvelled at their miniature glowing bodies. Before we closed the screen door to the blackness of the night, we opened our jars and let the minute lanterns carry their torches into the woods like aliens from another planet. In daytime, it was the butterfly hunt, capturing and releasing these flying wings of silk and colour. I even tried to desensitize myself to snakes by keeping a baby for a while. It would coil itself around my finger whenever I took it from its glass bowl. I never felt comfortable and soon released the snake to its rocky haven. Pet mice were another oddity I tried. I soon abandoned the idea, and I treat them more as pests than pets these days.

There were two dogs that have always been with me in thought and heart. Prince was a large shepherd/boxer cross mutt. He had a sandy-coloured, smooth coat with black points on his muzzle and ears distinguishing himself more like his shepherd parent. Prince lived outdoors in his insulated doghouse bedded deeply in golden straw. He was fastened by a chain and let off to run at least once per day.

Prince and I became inseparable buddies. Pretending that he was my horse, I once rigged up a harness and hooked him to a child's wagon. I then pointed him down the road. It was a sweltering day, and poor Prince had other ideas than pulling this kid around. Prince started out straight enough and began to imitate a canter down the bumpy dirt road. I had seemingly forgotten to invent a bridle for him. He wasn't very proficient in voice commands, either, but he knew the word "mush." Barrelling down the road at torpedo speed, Prince eyed the slow-running creek to his left. Pure thirst had overtaken any notion of going for a nice little jog down the country road. I had just enough time to bail when he took off over the bridge with the wagon in tow. It might have been a nasty landing had I not seen it coming and parted company. That was the end of my ingenious attempts to have a make-believe horse and cart.

It was another scorching Saturday with the Fahrenheit reaching well into the eighties. They say you could fry an egg on the blacktop. The air was stifling with no relief from any sort of faint breeze. I was swinging away, carefree and content, fanning my skin with the still air I disturbed with every push of my sandals. My parents were hunkered over as they cleared rock and debris, preparing the yard for seeding. My two brothers were in the house at the time; I'm not sure what they were doing. All I could hear was the thud of rocks piling into the wheelbarrow. A tall, strapping man appeared from the bush just behind my swing. I ran and told my dad that someone was coming. I thought it was strange, but since people often came to our house to have their televisions fixed, I didn't totally question his presence. Instinctively, Prince zeroed in on the stranger and started to sound alarm bells with a deep, long, and ferocious growl. The man made his way to the side of the house where the hose, still turned on, hung waiting to dampen the freshly raked soil. He ignored my father's queries. "What do you want?" my dad called out. Still there was no response. The man picked up the hose and dropped his head beneath its cool, showering relief from the baking sun. The dog continued his guard from the end of his chain becoming more animated. My dad walked toward the man, and then it happened.

Mom had her arms around my waist, clutching me close to her side as any protective parent would do. The stranger picked up a huge rock and held it over his head, threatening to hurl it at Mom and me. We were cornered against the wall of the house. He had us captive in his reach with the rock. Prince leapt from the end of his chain, snarling, his eyes ripe with fight; his hair bristled and stood at attention. Quick thinking was in order. Dad called to the intruder and demanded that he put the rock down, warning that he would otherwise suffer the consequences of Prince's wrath. The man looked at us, looked at the dog, and back again. It seemed like forever, but Dad's little psychology worked, and the man dropped the boulder and ran off down into the ravine and faded away in the distance. The police caught him the next day. We later learned that he was an escapee from the mental institution. Prince had become the hero and saved us from certain harm.

Prince

Prince's natural instinct to protect was later tested. This time, he bit a neighbour's daughter. The circumstances of the incident were unknown to us at the time. We later learned from a neighbour that the girl had taunted and hit him with a stick when he was chained. In his mind, his bite was a get-even response. Life seemed so unfair.

With the possibility of a lawsuit, Dad had no choice. I worshiped that dog that had literally saved my life. I planned to take the dog and hide out. I had packed supplies, such as a wool Hudson Bay blanket, matches, a little food, and a warm sweater to guard against the crisp fall air. I feared being alone in the woods at night as I started to reason with logic. Where could we go? Would we have enough food? What if the bears attacked us? There were just too many variables that could go wrong. I resigned myself to Prince's fate. I huddled in his doghouse, wrapping my arms around his neck and crying into his thick, soft coat. He cried, too, whining and licking my face as I sobbed. Soon Dad came with the rifle and took him for one last walk in the field high up on the hill. The crack of the rifle signalled that Prince's life was over. Dad didn't speak on his return. He had buried Prince in the meadow in which he'd loved to run. Dad made the solemn trek back alone. The sombre look on his face and the blank stare of his eyes said it all. Years later, I, too, would have to make a similar decision. I can now appreciate how much it must have hurt my dad.

Squeaky was a spaniel mix. She spent her daytime with us and went home at dinnertime. An older couple that lived just a few yards away were her legal guardians. She got her name because of her squeaky bark. She was such a patient, good-natured dog that I could do just about anything with her. She often took on the role as baby when I dressed her in doll clothes and put her in a doll carriage. She looked so adorable in her little hat and fancy clothes.

I had formed a little club with the younger boys in the neighbourhood, as I didn't have any girls to play with for quite some time. Still, my young lads tolerated me and joined in on my novel projects. I always managed to rope my little brother into all of my schemes.

We held our meetings in the sanctity of our attic. My dad had put in a disappearing staircase to the attic that worked on a series of weights. It was a perfect place to hold meetings; it was quiet and secret. When Squeaky needed an operation, we all banded together to discuss what we could do to help. It was decided that we would hold a rummage sale (similar to today's garage sales) and raise some money to purchase a dog coat. Since it was late fall, we figured

Chapter 5

Living in Suburbia

Those young days galloped by, and the years passed. It seemed an eternity to me, though, as it does for most children. My father made a life-changing decision to follow his dream and continue with his experimentation with long-distance television transmission. He had pioneered the cable television industry and set up the first system in the north. The mogul giant Famous Players wanted his lucrative territory and bought him out. It was the infancy of cable television and an industry that would revolutionize television. My father was a designer and inventor and now manufacturer of the parabolic antennas that would bring more programs into people's homes than ever before.

Later in 1964, we sold our lovely country home and moved south to Pickering, Ontario. My whole world seemed to have collapsed. It was all so different and foreign. To put it simply, I was miserable, angry, and despondent. I had left my only friends that I had grown up with, but more traumatizing was leaving behind the pony that had been my teacher, guardian of youth, and partner. I wasn't coping at all well in my new surroundings.

We had moved from the forestlands of the great north to a subdivision with its manicured lawns, paved streets, and night-lit roadways. I hated it with a passion. How could anyone call this living? I missed the north and all of its living creatures. I was a misfit. I was growing crazy from the withdrawal of country life. I continued with my collection of horse books, followed thoroughbred racing on television, and I constructed a scrapbook of newspaper clippings of some of my favourite racehorses.

I followed the racing career of the great Northern Dancer and his many rivals from beginning to end. At first, not always favoured, the press bestowed accolades on his challengers that included the Scoundrel, Quadrangle, and the heavy favourite for the Kentucky Derby, Hill Rise. They profiled these want-to-be Triple Crown hopefuls, splashing their pictures over the front pages of the sports section. The little Canadian horse that was sent back from the yearling sale unsold because of his diminutive size would later become the greatest sire of racehorses in the twentieth century. It was an exciting time for the sport of racing and Canadian breeders. It was a much-needed boost for the industry. Northern Dancer became a hero to his many Canadian racing fans. The gutsy bay stallion with the crooked blaze would become more famous at stud than during his stunning but brief racing career.

As I turned the musty, yellow, aged sheets of my scrapbook, the pages loose and dog-eared with time, a flood of memories filled the running video in my head. It took me back to that first Saturday afternoon in May 1964.

I sat cross-legged on the worn, carpeted floor in the living room, mesmerized by the live coverage of the Kentucky Derby as it played out on the black-and-white television set. I leaned forward and turned the knob up for full-volume effect. Perhaps a thousand miles away, I felt like I was in the grandstand listening to the hype and chatter of the excited throng of fans. The wicket agents passed out betting tickets in the flurry of wagers being placed before the monumental race. The television cameras panned the huge gathering crowd in the infield. It was standing room only, and even that was in short supply. I fantasized that I was among the ladies shaded from the hot Kentucky sun, dressed in their fancy hats and sipping cool mint juleps from fine crystal. It was a romantic tribute to another time as the grooms pampered their Kentucky Derby hopefuls and nostalgia trickled in with the crowds.

The twelve-horse field gave bettors a wide choice of favourites. Odds-on-favourite was Hill Rise, guided by "the Shoe," the great legendary Willy Shoemaker in the irons. My heart, of course, was betting on Northern Dancer and the accomplished jockey Bill Hartack.

As the field of horses for the Kentucky Derby stepped out into the bright sunshine and onto the racetrack, the crowd roared with approval, and the band began to play with sentiment, "My Old Kentucky Home." Northern Dancer strode out with his aristocratic head held high, exuding confidence. His head bobbed in anticipation of the starting gate. The nervous energy transformed the horses. Track goers and the many fans of racing were listening or watching from remote places. For the jockeys, this was the moment of focus, reflection, and steely nerves. I tilted forward, peering into the screen in an attempt to enlarge the image. I could envision the anxious torture of perspiration beading on their foreheads as the sweat trickled down the small channel of their tight spines. The jockeys took up rein and worked the track in warm-up mode. This was the appointed hour. The horses loaded one by one in the starting gate. The Dancer settled into the chute in the middle of the gate. The bell rang, and his powerful hindquarters dropped and drove forward as the horses sprang out of the gate and onto the open track. The race was on!

He wasn't the first horse to jump to the lead. Mr Brick took the early lead. Northern Dancer's competition was much taller as they strode ahead of the little fifteen-something-hand colt in the break from the gate. Still, I wasn't worried. I had faith in this smallish, fiery horse as I rocked back and forth on the floor, riding the race in spirit with his jockey. The announcer called out the names and positions as the horses settled into the run for the roses with the Dancer romping in seventh place just behind Hill Rise. The duelling horses jockeyed for position in this crowded field of contenders. I visualized the turquoise and gold silks of Windfields as the horses bunched together, rounding the track at the first turn. Inch by inch, Hartack skillfully moved the Dancer up to sixth place. I stayed fixated on saddlecloth number seven. I could easily pick out his left white fore as it stretched forward and pulled away at the dirt beneath him. The race not only depended upon the talent of the horse but also on the skill of the jockey. Manoeuvring a 1,000-pound thoroughbred pumping ahead at forty miles per hour on young, reckless legs in heavy traffic was no easy feat. Some of it depended on luck, but mostly it would be the experience of the tactical rider that would bring the horse home to the winner's circle.

Nearing the far turn, Hartack sends the Dancer after the leaders. With blistering speed, he begins to mow down his rivals in a cool, calculated drive for the lead. Quadrangle and Hill Rise follow closely in pursuit. From the outside, Northern Dancer drops into gear and challenges the three horses to his left. Like a bulldog, he flattens his frame and buries into his stride. Low and reaching, he slips by them until there is no one in front of him. He leads the pack in a determined drive. At the top of the stretch run, the Dancer pulls ahead. Shoemaker urges the California horse Hill Rise to press the Dancer as he lays his whip across the quarters to evoke more speed. The battle to the wire begins.

The little Canadian horse hangs tough and repels Hill Rise's advances. He digs deep into his reserve as Hartack's hands push harder and harder into his neck as he hand rides him forward. The crowd is now on its feet, urging the horses on as the finish line begins to close in on the rushing horses. Crumpled programs gripped in bettors' hands are punished against the railings as repeated blows mock the whipping fashion of the jockeys' crop. The fans hugging the rail scream at the top of their lungs, encouraging their horses to go farther and faster. I rock harder on the floor with each struggling stride. The gallop to the wire would place the favourites with Northern Dancer on the lead, followed by number eleven, Hill Rise, with the Scoundrel, Quadrangle, and Roman Brother in hot pursuit. The frantic battle for the blanket of roses ended as Northern Dancer crossed under the wire half a length ahead of Hill Rise in a track record-breaking time of two minutes flat! Northern Dancer would be the first Canadian-bred horse to win the Kentucky Derby, and he did it in style. The fans went wild! I went wild! History had been made as the mighty little horse from Oshawa, Ontario, trotted into the winner's circle, and the blanket of roses was laid across his wispy withers. Northern Dancer stood proudly basking in the glory as the hero of the moment. Jubilant tears rolled down my cheeks in utter elation and pride. My little thoroughbred horse had won and had proved his doubters wrong!

I turned the pages and replayed the Dancer's subsequent races, including the Preakness.

The second jewel in the Triple Crown placed Northern Dancer as a favourite. The six-horse field engaged some of the Kentucky Derby entries, including his old rivals Hill Rise and Quadrangle. The public was unaware that the Dancer running on a hoof with a quarter crack that had been temporarily patched for the race. There were no guarantees that this repair would hold under a severe drive in the race. A patch had never been attempted before. Still, Northern Dancer showed no lameness as he leaped into third position when the gate swung wide. By the final turn, Northern Dancer had taken the lead from the remaining challenger and galloped under the wire all alone.

His defeat in the Belmont when he agonizingly lost room on the rail to run denied him the Triple Crown. It would be Quadrangle's day, and Northern Dancer's hopes of a Triple Crown win were dashed.

I turned another page in the scrapbook journal. The next news clips depicted a returning champion as Northern Dancer sailed over the finish line. He was seven-and-a-half lengths ahead of Langcrest in the 1964 Queen's Plate. Royalty honoured the little bay stallion that day. The victory presentation was made to his jubilant owner E P Taylor by none other than the Queen Mum herself.

The traditional fifty gold sovereign guinea purse established by King Charles I in 1663, was later substituted for a silver plate by King Charles II in the seventeenth century. Queen Victoria gave her royal blessing for the first Queen's Plate on June 27, 1860. Today the Queen's Plate is no longer fifty gold sovereign guineas, or a silver plate. Instead it is a foot high gold cup.

A few more gallery pages flipped by, honouring past champions. The pages were filled with old press clippings of Titled Hero, Viceregal, Dancer's Image, and the gallant Cool Reception. Cool Reception galloped under the wire on three legs in second place, only to be destroyed later when a failed attempt to save his broken leg ended in tragedy.

It is time to come back to the present time. As I rest the scrapbook on the coffee table, a decaying newspaper clipping falls to the floor. I retrieve the archival piece and open the folds with care. The headlines bring a heaviness of grief as it announces in bold print "**Sadness Grips Windfields Farm as Legendary Northern Dancer Dies,**" Saturday, November 17, 1990, in the *Oshawa Times*. I reverently return the folds and rest the tired newsprint in the scrapbook. I had enjoyed my visit with the past, enriching my life with its occasions of thrill and cheer and even melancholy. Racing truly is a heartbreaking sport.

The only good thing about moving to a more so-called civilized culture was being able to watch multiple channels on television. Although I loved my native town dearly, it was stagnant in the world of entertainment as far as young people were concerned. What kid wanted to tune in to *Don Messer's Jubilee*? The only real excitement on television was *Hockey Night in Canada* during the winter months and of course *The Ed Sullivan Show* and the Western series *Bonanza* on Sunday nights. When the weather conditions were right and Dad's antenna was at its peak performance, we could pull in some of the United States' stations, albeit fuzzy at times. The black-and-white tube sets were the norm, as colour television hadn't yet been invented. It was then that I got to see shows like *Mr. Ed*, *The Lone Ranger*, *Roy Rogers*, and others. I watched the movie *My Friend Flicka* and John Steinbeck's tragic tale *The Red Pony*. I still remember the tears trickling down my cheek, washing away the final scene as the pony died.

One of my favourite movie characters was Francis a talking mule. The first film debuted in 1950 simply titled *Francis*. Six hysterically funny sequels followed. The movies included *Francis Goes to the Races*, *Frances Goes to West Point*, *Francis Covers the Big Town*, *Francis Joins the WACS*, *Francis in the Navy*, and finally *Francis in the Haunted House*. By giving the mule a voice, it humanized it. Perhaps it wasn't far from the truth if indeed horses (mules) could speak our dialect.

All the local radio station played was the twang of the original country music. I loathed it. Country music today is nothing like it was then. Granted, it was popular, but not with me. This was the era of the Beatles, Elvis, and the Rolling Stones!

When we relocated to southern Ontario, my parents tried enrolling me in riding lessons. A very prestigious riding academy in Toronto's north-west end was willing to take me under its wing. Logistically, it was too far for my parents to drive me on a regular basis. Most of the Olympic hopefuls trained there, and I was a little disappointed that I couldn't have the discipline and instruction I so longed for. My parents finally settled on a riding school that was a little closer but still a distance from our home. I attempted riding my bicycle there for a lesson. After three hours on the bike, I was exhausted and barely able to sit in the saddle. I needed a ride home as my oxygen-deprived legs were rubbery, and I dreaded the long climb up the valley on the Rouge River thoroughfare.

I took lessons for the remainder of the summer but was never comfortable with the instructor. We did plenty of drill work and hard riding. It strengthened my position and gave me better balance. One of the instructors put me up on their good horse, a lovely palomino mare named Honey. I still hadn't mastered the art of leg aids or seat position with proficiency. I remember Honey picked up the canter when I accidentally shifted my hip, and off we went. The more I gripped, the faster she ran. I felt totally out of control. I remember hearing the young instructor shouting at me to stop gripping and release. There was no way I was letting go! Lap after lap, we churned up the dirt of the ring. I think I tired the poor horse out as she finally broke to a trot. Her sides ballooned outward with the heavy heaving and wild panting of her flared nostrils. I never rode Honey again. I needed more skill before I tackled another ride on this fine-tuned horse.

My regular instructor owned the riding stable. He was an old military coach who, although a good disciplinarian, had a demented fancy streak for young girls. He always had his favourites, and I never felt comfortable waiting for my ride home in his house. He was too friendly for my liking, and my intuition told me to leave. I would steal myself away, discouraging his advances. Instead, I chose to wait at the end of the long, tree-lined driveway for my dad to pick me up. This would not be my first encounter with a sexual predator in my young life and the connection to stables. As I learned, horses could also be used as an effective lure to target the many naïve girls who hung around stables. These perpetrators could trap these young females in uncomfortable and frightening situations. It was the small but insidious side of the horse world that would haunt me for the rest of my life.

Chapter 6

A Horse of My Own

I was just starting my teen years and beginning high school. The hormones shaped my future, along with a myriad of health problems that would plague me the rest of my life. I suffered from chronic anaemia and required regular monitoring and painful iron injections. The one undeviating focal point through all of these life-altering changes—including an allergy to horses, no less—was my desire to own my own horse. It wasn't going to be a passing fancy that many young girls grow out of. This was a permanent addiction.

My parents were concerned with my unhappiness. One day at dinner, my father became so frustrated with my downcast demeanour and constant gloom that he thought he might try to shake me out of it. I received a hard slap across my face. It didn't work; it only tormented me all the more. Resolving themselves to the fact that their daughter needed a horse in her life, they broke the news to me. I was elated! The cloud of despair lifted, and I began to enjoy life again. At last, I would have a horse I could call my own. There were strings attached, but nothing was going to stop me now, not even the allergist's recommendation that I stay away from horses. I was determined. My parents liked what they saw when I was with a horse.

It was not only the nurturing side but also the degree of responsibility and positive attitude that came with it. By far, the horse was safer than boys. My mother believed that horses were a godsend during the often troubling times of adolescent years.

My parents were willing to cut a deal with me. They would purchase the horse, but the financial commitment from then on was my sole responsibility. Buying the horse, of course, is the least expensive proposition of owning a horse. But I was determined not to fail, and I didn't. I babysat every weekend to earn enough money to pay for the horse's board, farrier, and veterinary bills. Only once in all the years did my parents have to help me out. It was a pretty good record given that I was only fourteen at the time. I never regretted having the horse, missing out on dates, or not being able to afford fashionable clothes. I was richer than I had ever been, and I was thankful.

Dad and I started the hunt for a horse. We travelled to the Stouffville area, where a load of mustangs from western Canada had arrived and were being readied for sale. They were indeed a wild and rough-looking string that belonged more in the rodeo than in someone's backyard. I picked out a little black yearling filly and had my heart set on her. She ran around the box stall, her eyes wide with panic. Dad wasn't convinced it was a good choice and neither was the seller. We went home empty-handed but with more horses to see another day. Hope reigned eternal.

I had walked through so many paddocks and looked at so many horses that I became very impatient and disillusioned. It was a Sunday morning when Dad put down the receiver after taking down directions to a farm in Newcastle, Ontario. It seemed like such a long drive. I wasn't holding out much hope of finding a horse. We arrived at the farm shortly after lunch and walked through the overgrazed field. The owner pointed out to a herd of young, recently trained horses he had for sale. There was a little of everything, and they all seemed like sensible mounts. In the centre of the group was a tall, refined palomino. He caught my eye immediately. I asked to see him. He wore a simple rope halter, and he sniffed my outstretched hand as he approached me. He had a pretty head and kind, soft brown eyes. His mane was of medium length, and his tail was long and flowing with strands of white. His coat was a pale gold colour but handsome just the same. I knew that this horse was the one.

This special horse had to have an equally impressive name. I called him Magnificent (a.k.a. Mags) and later added on the rest... the Magician. I had found a small stable between the high school I attended and home. It was a perfect arrangement, as I could visit my horse every day on the way home from school. The people raised beagles, so my horse soon got used to the dog kennels and noise. There was another horse for company that belonged to the owner's son. Brandy was a flashy-coloured paint and a good companion for Mags. I was now living my dream.

Magnificent and friends

I found an old cavalry saddle that was for sale. It was $35, and I had just enough in my budget. It wasn't the most comfortable saddle with its steel tree and worn leather. At least it was better than bareback, and I could practice my equestrian skills on it. I was given an old bridle with a loose ring snaffle. It would do.

I rode every day and got to know my horse that first year. We racked up a lot of miles on the washboard roads. My gelding responded to my directions, and we advanced enough to enter the occasional show. At 16.2 hands, he was impressive. His freshly minted gold coat and pure silk white mane and tail made him a knockout in the ring. We stuck to the English pleasure and trail classes, winning ribbons. I was so proud of our team effort. I practised jumping, starting with the cavalettis[6] and working my way up until we cleared five feet. That was getting a bit too much toward the heavens, and I didn't want to visit that place any time soon. I dropped down to the hunter level, and that's where we stayed.

Mags was very wise and took care of me in times of danger. On one occasion, my dad came to watch me jump a few poles in the field. My timing was off when I turned and faced the fence at a canter. Mags attempted to jump off stride from about four feet away. He hooked one front leg over the bar and the other leg under. He somersaulted in a huge ball with flaying hooves, mane, and tail. We hit the ground hard. My dad was speechless and horrified as he watched the events unfold. Mags took a moment to sort out his legs before righting himself and standing up. He carefully placed his hooves on either side of my crumpled-up body. When he rose, I was lying directly underneath him. He never moved until I rolled myself out from beneath him. Dad kept shaking his head in amazement. To think a horse would take such care not to injure its rider truly amazed to him.

As time passed, I decided to relocate my horse to another stable where I could be in close proximity to the school. It allowed me to continue my daily visits. There was some land owned by a couple that

---

6   Cavelletis are poles raised off the ground and spaced apart so a horse can trot over them, lifting its feet and developing balance and cadence.

kept a horse close by. Dad had permission to erect a small building to house my horse. We bought a prefabricated garage directly from the factory and had the doors modified. It came one day, and when it was assembled, I had a cute, dry stable. My horse had a huge stall with windows to watch over his pasture. He seemed to thrive there, and we continued our daily hacks out in the country.

I had a change of clothes with me, and I would strip down in the barn to begin my chores and go for a quick ride before heading home for supper. Since Mags was a great escape artist (hence the lengthening of his name to Magnificent the Magician), I got into the practice of tethering him in his stall. No matter what latch we tried, he eventually knew how to open it. He would pay attention to our actions and then copy them or at least fiddle until he got the combination right. The road leading from the house was a busy highway. I didn't want any accidents, so securing him in the stable was a must for Magnificent the Magician.

I received an urgent phone call one Sunday morning from the owners of the property. My horse had some terrible lacerations, and my lovely little stable was in shambles. My dad rushed me over to see what could be done. The veterinarian was summoned. When we arrived and looked into the building, it was like a tornado had ripped through the heart of my quaint little barn. High up in the rafters of the building, we discovered the source of this disaster. The culprit was a large, angry hornets' nest. Somehow, my horse had disturbed them, and they attacked with a vicious vengeance. He had been stung over and over as he tried to escape his tormentors. Boards were kicked out, scattering like matchstick pieces. Huge porthole-type openings were left in its wake. All of the window panes were shattered. Blood was splashed on the walls as though a loose can of red paint had sprayed them indiscriminately. The tethering rope had been cut to free my frantic horse. He had an odd twist to his muzzle. This resulted in paralysis from the prolonged tight hold of the rope. It had cut off circulation long enough to cause nerve damage. I was horrified to see my horse in such a state. The veterinarian arrived to stitch up his wounds. The face was another problem. He advised me that the nerves might regenerate over time with daily massages to the area. The scepticism that a young girl of my age would have the patience and devotion to nurse the horse on a daily basis was so visible on his face that it only reinforced my fortitude and determination to prove him wrong in his assumptions. He couldn't guarantee any success in having the muzzle return to a normal position even with regular massages. I was advised that the disfigurement might be permanent.

I felt a profound sense of guilt for putting my horse in harm's way and not being more vigilant about the maintenance of the stable. If I had been more observant, perhaps I would have seen the nest before it became a real problem. Perhaps?

The long process of healing began. Regardless of the weather, I kept up the daily massage for about six months. The treatment paid off; eventually, the nerve responses returned, and the muzzle straightened. The sutures came out without any residual scarring; we were lucky. The owners of the property didn't want the responsibility for another person's horse anymore, so we were on the move again looking for a stable.

For a brief time, I boarded my horse with a boyfriend who had a horse named Jubal. We had great fun riding together. Harold was a tall boy with a brawny build. A few scrawny whiskers started to protrude from his boyish, soft skin, adding a wisp of manliness to his rugged, outdoorsy appearance. He always liked to show off with his horse and gallop by me. Jubal was a tough little horse that could spin on a dime and work a Western rein with ease. Harold's bravado would land him in some serious trouble.

We started out for a nice summer ride down the dust-choked road. Harold decided that he wanted to race, but I was reluctant, as my horse wasn't shod. "Suit yourself," he teased. He spurred his horse on with gusto and left me behind as his voice trailed off in the distance, still enticing me to follow. I'm sure it skipped his joyride mind that this dirt road melted into a slick paved road with a decisive curve that screamed caution. Running flat out, Jubal's hooves dug in and pounded hard against the dry-packed road. It was too late for Harold to take up rein. They hit the pavement at full speed while attempting to navigate the sharp turn. All I could see were sparks shooting from Jubal's steel shoes; it was a grand fireworks display. As the sparks continued, the horse's legs skidded out from beneath him. He fell with an awful thud to the blacktop. I jogged up to survey the damage. At first, I was shocked, but then I was relieved to see both rider and horse seemingly unscathed. I was laughing so hard I thought I was going to roll out of the saddle seeing Harold sitting in the middle of the deserted road. His horse grazed contently at the side of the road. Harold picked himself up, clutching his left arm in utter agony. "I think I broke my arm," he complained. The expression on his face was no longer one of glee. Instead, he grimaced with pain as he picked up the ends of his horse's reins. We walked the horses back to the stable. It was a rather quiet walk home, as what seemed a foolish venture on the part of my He-Man boyfriend left him with a broken wing and a tarnished ego. I didn't have the heart to say, "I told you so." The next day, Harold showed up at school sporting a fresh white cast on his arm. We continued our on-again, off-again friendship for a few more months. It was time to move on.

I met a young girl named June Gillespie. She had a spunky little chestnut Morgan gelding that she showed in hunt classes. June was a very talented rider who had made the big times in the world of hunters, showing at the Royal Winter Fair and other big events. An only child, June was the pride and joy of her parents. She was provided with the finest in equestrian wear and equipment. How I envied her. She was a year or two younger than I, but we got along splendidly despite the age difference.

At the time, I had an interest in the sport of long-distance riding. I had a game plan for conditioning my horse sufficiently to enter a 25-mile ride in late spring. I rode several miles every day. I thought it might be a useful tool if I could gauge the speed of his different gaits. In theory, it wasn't a bad idea. I asked my dad if he could follow me in the car and note the speed at which my horse trotted and cantered. Off we went to a long section of gravel road that lacked regular traffic. With the calling of spring, my horse had begun the heavy shedding of his winter woollies. I had encouraged a hasty conclusion to this rite of spring with the use of body clippers. I had saddled my horse using the normal billet[7] placing of the girth. I hadn't allowed for the lack of hair as I placed the saddle pad on the shaven coat. This would be a devastating error in judgment.

I began a slow, calculated trot down the lone road. The only sound that broke the still air that early afternoon was the hollow thud of my horse's hooves contacting the road, followed by the crackle of gravel beneath the car's tires. The engine hummed quietly with the low engine revolutions registering on the tachometer. My father and mother followed at a safe distance behind me, noting the speed at which I was travelling. I pushed my horse up a notch and extended the length of his stride. I still wasn't aware that the saddle was slowly edging its way to the right side of the horse. It wasn't until I slipped my horse into the canter that things started to fall apart.

The rock of this slow gallop pushed my saddle way off centre with each roll forward. I lost my left stirrup. The detachment from my boot caused the stirrup iron to pound the side of my horse with every stride. It was just as if a jockey was going to the whip with the finish line in view. Faster and faster, my horse drove forward with a sudden burst of speed. I desperately tried to right the saddle by forcing all of my weight to the left, supported by the one remaining stirrup. It was all in vain. In a matter of seconds, I was hurtling down

7   Billets are the leather straps that the girth is attached to that hold the saddle in place.

in slow motion from the back of my horse. With each leaping stride, I edged closer to the ground, hanging upside down. I was dangling precariously from the stubborn stirrup. The saddle continued to rotate to the right. I soon realized my fate of crashing into the hard-packed dirt at breakneck speed. The whirl of the dirt and dust from the galloping charger beckoned me closer. That gift of a helmet so long ago would be tested. It encased my head, muffling the rapid blows as they glanced off the helmet. I slid at an awkward angle with my one foot hanging from the still secure stirrup. I hit the ground headfirst and remained conscious for three or four seconds as my helmet bounced like a beach ball. The horse's hooves brushed by the helmet as he raced on. The stirrup finally released, and my limp body lay still in the settling dust. My horse continued his gallop toward the elusive finish line.

I recall seeing only blue sky and experiencing a horrible ringing in my ears. I rolled my head to the side and saw the tread of the tires rushing toward me. I couldn't move and prayed briefly that they wouldn't run over me. My mother, hysterical with panic, flung the door open before the car came to a full stop and began running toward me, screaming my name. As I moaned in pain, my dad picked me up and laid me with great care on the backseat of the car. He was cool under pressure; he drove fast but carefully.

We arrived at the hospital, and I was admitted to the intensive care unit, where I remained for forty-eight hours. I thought my head was going to explode. I had the worst headache imaginable with a fresh line of stitches in my scalp. The doctors told me that the helmet had saved my life. The ankle that was trapped in the stirrup would never be strong again, as it had been stretched beyond normalcy. My legs and arms were cleansed and dressed with bandages and soothing creams. The ghoulish-looking abrasions were deep.

All I could think about that first night in intensive care was who would look after my horse if I died. I prayed in earnest that the dear

Lord would not allow my parents to grieve for their daughter. The room was filled with beeping monitors, tubes, rushing doctors, and nurses, and there were several other patients in there with me. One patient hadn't made it, and I didn't want to be next. I had too much more to do in my young life, and I was so frightened.

The days dragged on. Each day, I held the hope that I would be released from this prison of white with its sterile floors and meals of bland, tasteless food and jelly desserts. The nights and mornings blended together. It was boring and only got worse as I continued to heal. I longed for the comfort of my own bed and a night not interrupted with thermometers, blood pressure cuffs, and nurses holding my wrist in the early hours of the morning. It had been close to ten days before I was allowed to leave the ward. An attendant pushed my wheelchair down the hall and out under the canopy of the main entrance. At last I was going home.

It was good to be home. I had missed my room, my family, and my horse. I had only been home for a couple of days when my dad handed me a new helmet and announced that we were going to the stable. My horse had wandered home the day of the accident and was enjoying a holiday out on the grass while my wounds healed. My dad drove up the secluded lane lined with full pine and maple trees that led to the stable. He patiently waited for me to tack up my horse before instructing me to mount up. He knew from his own personal experiences, one being a near-fatal motorcycle crash, that the most important thing to do is to face your fear, and the sooner the better. With apprehension clearly displayed in a fearful frown on my face, I pushed off the ground and rested quietly in the saddle. It was good to be back even though I only walked the ring and trotted small circles. It would take several rides before I would finally feel comfortable at the canter again, but I would eventually recover both physically and with renewed confidence. Today, the girth of my saddle is checked at least four times before I mount up, with the horse being walked several minutes beforehand. Being dragged down a dirt road by a galloping horse was surely a lesson out of the curriculum from the School of Hard Knocks.

School vacations in the summer were always met with enthusiasm. My father had built a roomy, single-horse trailer that could be hitched to our station wagon. The maiden trip took me home to the north to visit my childhood playground. Mags stayed at the very stable I grew up with as I rode the not-so-familiar dirt road that was now blacktop. The swamp that I had taken shortcuts through in the winter months was now a massive community of brick dwellings. The wetland was gone, and so was the wilderness beauty. I rode Mags up to our old neighbours who remained with the changing scenery all those years. They welcomed me like a sister that had been away for a long time. It was good to come home. I had missed my childhood fortress of timber and rock. The draw of the north is still strong for me with its wilderness calls and changes of season.

A second vacation took me to my grandmother's cottage on the shores of Rice Lake. A neighbouring farmer allowed me to keep my horse in his cow barn for the week while we were vacationing. Every day, I saddled up and rode out, exploring the terrain and back roads. My horse and I had formed an unbreakable bond by now. It was like practising mental telepathy as we navigated pathways without a word. We were true partners. I pretty much just thought the instructions to my horse, and he would respond.

During one of my daily explorations, I travelled down a closed, unapproved road that led to an old weatherworn wooden bridge. The bridge spanned a small creek bed. I didn't fancy testing the solidness of the bridge atop my 1,100-pound horse, so I briefly surveyed the innocent-looking watershed below. Mags would go anywhere I asked him, as he trusted my judgment. On this occasion, my judgment would prove to be flawed as he stepped into a deep bog that swallowed him up quickly. He struggled to lift his enormous body from the bottomless muck. Inch by inch, he sank farther and farther as I attempted to turn him back toward the security of the bank. He heaved in vain until the saddle was swallowed up in the brown soup. I slipped off his back to lighten his load and lay on my stomach. I began dog paddling to the edge of the bank with reins in hand. With only a portion of his neck and head poking out from the quicksand, he moaned in defeat. It was a resonating sound of despair I had never heard him utter before.

I tried not to panic as the tears started to trickle down my taut cheeks as the realization that he might die in the swamp started to sink in. I pulled myself together, as all the weeping in the world wouldn't help me rescue my horse. Knowing that Mags would try his best for me, I pleaded with him to move toward the bank. It was only a couple of feet to freedom. I needed him to muster enough strength to push his huge bulk through the quagmire. I let him rest for a minute or two, and then I called to him, "Come on, boy. Come on." His ears pricked forward, and his soft, trusting eyes reflected back into my anxious dry eyes. He lunged forward, took a deep breath, and expelled the air with a deep, mournful groan. He lifted his entire shoulders up as the toe of his unshod hooves dug into the grassy bank. "That's a boy, come on," I pleaded again. Somehow, Mags found the strength for the final push forward as he slid to his knees and managed to find some grip. He scrambled on to the knoll in a muddy heap.

Mags rose to his feet. His sides heaved from exhaustion as he hung his head. I patted his neck and praised him for his courage. We both stank from the rotting vegetation of the swamp. I had thought it was such a peaceful-looking stream, but death lurked below its tranquil beauty. I turned Mags away from the deadly suction of the creek. I walked beside him as I led him back to the farm and his stall in the cow barn. After telling my story to the local farmer, he told me that a cow had been lost at that same spot a few years before. We had been fortunate to survive the pull of the mud. I washed the stench and slimy camouflage from his golden coat and snow-coloured tail and mane.

Back home again, June Gillespie was getting taller in her adolescent years. She was outgrowing her game little Morgan and preparing for the bigger leagues. In anticipation of her advancement in equitation, her parents purchased her a three-year-old thoroughbred gelding fresh off the racetrack. June began working with it, grooming it for future competition as a potential jumper. She was aiming for an upcoming local show and only had a matter of weeks to get the horse accustomed to reaching high instead of bolting from a starting gate. June rode every day. She slowed the gallop to a canter and relaxed the horse. She worked the cavalettis while setting some small jumps and flying the thoroughbred gelding over them with ease. I followed behind, jumping Mags over the small course of oxers and spread jumps. The rolling hills made an ideal event course with elevation to gallop and valleys to shorten and collect the horse's overall body frame.

The day of the show approached. June and I shipped out for the big event. She entered a few more hunter classes than I did. I was content to do the English pleasure and one hunt course. As our class approached, a few riders were called ahead of us. Wearing a nervous smile on our lips, we wished each other luck. We had our strategies planned for our horses to cover the course cleanly and in a timely fashion. The obstacles weren't terribly large fences, but they were unforgiving solid fences. Any miscalculation could spell disaster for a rider. June's number was called, and I was listed on deck. I was eager to see how she paced her new horse over this course. Her Morgan had done these same events for years and always sailed over the fences with ease, usually bringing home a red ribbon and trophy at the end of the competition. June really wanted her new horse to shine. However, this was not her Morgan but an untested ex-racer that was still unfamiliar with the sport of eventing and hunt. His tall, leggy frame should have allowed him to conquer any of the rails without breaking into lather or rubbing a pole. June guided him to the first fence, which was a simple rail. He bounded over it with a foot of air to spare. Next was a brush fence. The big, galloping thoroughbred stood back and leaped over the fence boldly. *He should make a good jumper*, I thought as he started burning up the turf. June checked him back and swung around for the stone wall. She put her horse center to the fence and galloped forward. Courage escaped him as he approached the wall, and he drove his front hooves into the ground, aborting the takeoff. The sudden breaking action catapulted June over his head with great force, and she hit the wall at 30 miles per hour. The reins were still in her grip as she plunged sideways into the wall, catching the big thoroughbred off balance. He fell heavily, pinning June against the stone fence. She never moved! People rushed to her aid as the horse struggled to its feet. An ambulance rushed in as it bumped its way through the rough field. The attendants worked on her, placing her shattered little body on to a striker board. They loaded her in the vehicle and headed out with sirens blaring en route to the nearest hospital.

I was stunned. I prayed she would be okay. The show resumed, and I was next up. "Please, St Christopher, give me a safe ride," I pleaded skyward. My confidence had been shaken. My horse refused the first fence. I withdrew from the competition. Our ride wasn't at all like we had rehearsed. I kept seeing images of June being crushed against that stone wall. My focus was gone, and Mags instinctively felt my insecurity about the ride.

The next morning, I heard the terrible news. June had died that night, unable to regain consciousness. Rumours said that her father was so grief-stricken that he shot the horse that night. June's death tore the family apart. I never jumped again.

I moved my horse once more to a large riding stable in Pickering. When I reached my sixteenth birthday, I applied for my driver's licence and got it on my first attempt. Dad gave me use of the old station wagon. I now had wheels and independence. No longer did I have to rely on someone else's goodwill to drive me to the barn. No more long, boring waits for a ride to come. I was happy to have a vehicle even if it wasn't sporty. Over the course of the next few years, I became a sponge soaking up everything about horses that I could.

I observed and assisted with the treatment of sick and injured horses at the stable.

I saw many ailments and diseases at that stable. Most of the tired old horses were used as school or trail mounts. One poor gelding had heaves (emphysema) so badly that he kept falling over in his stall from lack of oxygen as the large abdominal muscle tried to push the air from his lungs. The owner finally had the horse put down for humane reasons.

I witnessed laminitis and the cruel ravages and pain this hoof disease inflicts on a horse. My horse became mysteriously ill, too. He took to staggering fits. The veterinarian was stymied and suggested that it could be a result of small strongi, more commonly known as blood worms, travelling through the bloodstream and reaching the delicate brain tissue. In those days, we only dewormed a horse for parasites twice a year. Horses had a stomach tube inserted by a veterinarian in which the medication was administered. There wasn't the variety of parasite control products that are available today. Eventually, the problem resolved itself, and Mags returned to a steady gait. It was during this time that I purchased a second horse.

He was a big-boned palomino that I named Whisper. He was an excellent saddle horse and could jump. I had purchased him from a dealer, and after a short period of time, I discovered my prize gelding had a condition known as shivers. The problem persisted only when picking out the hind hooves. He would tuck his leg high underneath himself and shake for several seconds before relaxing the leg. It never seemed to affect his gait when riding, but it was more of a nuisance during grooming.

One of the favourite horses at the stable was a darling old pony named Pat. He was a dark bay who did just about anything for his young owner. The tall lad named John was inseparable from his pony. John rode the willing pony on the bridle paths nearly every day. He worked the barrels and flagpole course, practicing his gaming skills. He rode him bareback and swam the tributaries of the slow-moving river that rambled through the pasturelands at the north end of the property. John always had a tired smile on his face as he held the end of the reins and let Pat stretch into the retirement of the ride. Pat always obliged his rider's wishes, always with his ears pointing forward with interest.

They found poor Pat lying in the field one morning, suspecting that his old ticker gave out during the night. The boy took the news hard. John ran as fast as he could through the spotty weed pasture of late August. He called for Pat between the tears that rained down his cheeks. He leaned over the cold, dead pony and sobbed into its long, black mane that once flew with the wind. It was a sobering moment as they winched old Pat into a dead stock truck. I never saw his owner again. The sacred communion between horse and rider had been broken. I, too, would grieve for the loss of a horse one day and could only imagine the suffering this young boy felt. I dreaded the day it would be my turn.

Chapter 7

Buenos Dias

When I turned eighteen, I landed my first job after graduating from high school. I started saving for a holiday of a lifetime. I found an advertisement in an equestrian magazine for a riding adventure in Spain. I noted the address and corresponded. It was described as an exciting ride in the old southern region of Spain. A prerequisite to the ride was a requirement that all equestrians have a minimum of seven years of riding experience. I was young, full of enthusiasm, and ready to take on the mountains of Spain. Little did I know how relevant the experience requirement would be.

I decided to indulge myself in some culture before packing my brand-new Carson luggage and flying off to this European destination. I had a Spanish translation book that I studied from cover to cover. I noted the important dietary words like *pollo*, or chicken, my favourite diet. I memorized numbers *uno, dos,* etc., that I thought might come in handy. I learned *caballo*, which translates to horse. I purchased the now extinct, long-playing vinyl records. The 33 $^{1/3}$ whirled away to the haunting melodies of a classical Spanish guitar as the needle followed the tracks with each revolution of the turntable. My passport was in order, and I was on my way.

I had never been overseas or travelled solely on my own before then. To say that I wasn't a little anxious would be an untruth. However, the thought of riding a handsome Andalusian horse in the mountains of Alora allayed any fears I might have had.

My parents were excited for me if not a touch worried. They drove me to the airport and helped me get settled before the flight left. I had to change planes in New York, and from there it was a straight run to Malaga, Spain. It would be a long flight in the cramped confines of the old Boeing 707 with its three seats tucked stubbornly close in a row. I tossed about in the seat trying to find a comfort position so that I could drift off for an hour or so. It was impossible. It was a terribly long and boring flight. This was pre-VCR and DVD days with no entertainment other than a day-old newspaper or a good novel that one carried on board. I waited so long that I was desperate to make an unbalanced trip to the closet-sized washroom. I decided to head for the front section just behind the cockpit. The door was closed, and the sign partially read *Occupied*. I waited patiently, looking at the carpet and then up at the ceiling and back at the carpet again. *Boy, someone must have a real problem,* I thought to myself. *What could be taking so long?* I started squirming a bit as the minutes dragged on. My fidgeting produced some curious looks from the flight attendants. This was the era of hijackers. I think their suspicious glances were starting to put me into that category. Finally, one of the flight attendants stepped forward and asked me if she could be of assistance. I sheepishly replied in an almost inaudible voice that I was waiting for the washroom. They decided to investigate and rapped on the door. There was no reply. By now, the whole plane of passengers had their eyes glued on me. I felt like I could have crawled into the cargo hold of the plane and disappeared from sight. The mystery was solved. No one was in the washroom, and the latch had not been returned to its appropriate position, obscuring the *Occupied* sign. I quickly dashed in, shutting the small door behind me while ensuring the signage was clearly visible. I sighed with relief. Now all I had to do was to make the trip back to my seat without being detected.

The dark, oceanic skies gave way to the early dawn of tomorrow. Seven hours after leaving New York, I arrived to bright sunshine on the coastal port of Malaga. The immigration officer stamped my passport as I made my way with the rest of the passengers who had disembarked from the plane. A slender woman wearing a crisp cotton dress held a large sign over her head in the arrivals waiting area. My name was inscribed on the sign. I approached her and introduced myself. She welcomed me to Spain and helped me load my luggage into her small sedan. Deprived of sleep, I was running on adrenaline.

Spain

We left the seaside town of Malaga and headed up the mountain range to the village. This would be our base camp for the holiday on horseback. The small car rounded each bend in the narrow road as my hostess levelled her hand on the horn with deliberation. She explained that it was imperative to warn other motorists and donkey cart drivers that you were rounding a curve. The roads were too narrow to pass safely. My guide pointed out the caves high in the hills where the gypsies made temporary lodgings. I was promptly advised never to engage these people in a conversation or acknowledge them in any way. There had been several incidents of thievery and even murder. It wasn't a reassuring conversation, but I was captive in the sputtering car that was leading me farther from civilization.

We finally arrived at a lovely, centuries-old villa. I was shown to a large room with the shades drawn to blacken it. The slate floor was cool and the spacious room devoid of a lot of furniture. I wanted to sleep forever and just about did. I remember someone knocking loudly at my door the next morning. I had slept an entire day!

At breakfast that morning, I was reintroduced to our hostess, the same woman who had read me the riot act about avoiding the wandering gypsies. She was a gracious and cultured woman. She always dressed with femininity, and her long, blonde tresses that often overflowed her slender shoulders were tied and pinned with every hair in place. She spoke seven languages fluently and was able to converse with people on an intellectual level. She was also our translator while on tour and a consummate rider, as well. I soon met the group of equestrians with whom I would be travelling. It was a multicultural mix of nations representing a global community of riders. There were German, British, American, and Italian members, and, of course, yours truly, the only Canadian and youngest member of the tour. We were formally introduced to our official guide and the owner of the villa.

Antonio was obviously from an aristocratic family of the village. He held the title of marquis, a rank bestowed to elite members of society, surpassed in title only by the title of duke. He was considered a nobleman.

All the villagers revered him. He was a dark-haired Spaniard in his early thirties whose tanned, rugged good looks and slim body reminded me of the movie matinee idol who played the part of Zoro. Antonio led us through some awesome country over the course of ten days as we rode from village to village in the high, mountainous terrain. The paths we took brought us by the ancient stone arenas of the matadors. We rode through the tiered hillsides of bountiful orange groves whose strong scent drifted in the light breeze of elevation. Miles of stubborn needlepoint cactus and protruding rock would ensure full attention as we rolled in the saddle.

On the first day of our equestrian adventure, we were individually assigned our purebred Andalusian horses. Grooms had the horses prepared and saddled. We mounted and rode through the village and out into the countryside. It was a "get-acquainted" ride, and it was our only opportunity to trade mounts for the remainder of the tour if we so wished and the other rider agreed.

Being more limber and the youngest rider, I was given a bold and sturdy grey gelding named Romero. Fresh from castration, Romero still harboured some strong hormones that lingered and manifested themselves in rank stallion behaviour. His beautiful crest arched in glorious dignity, unaware of his lost manhood, as he pranced along the cobblestone of the village courtyard. It was a circus atmosphere as the villagers gathered to watch the spectacle of horse and foreign rider parade through the ancient square. The steel shoes on the horses' hooves slid precariously on the polished cobblestone. The horses nervously tap danced along the narrow streets. My four-year-old's testosterone levels still burned in his muscles, giving him that touch of arrogance. He popped and bucked with exuberance that first ride, so much so that no one would trade mounts with me at the end of the day. He settled for a brief period of time, allowing me to relax and take in the sensuous, tangy fragrance of sweet orange groves.

As we plodded along the narrow path, all of us took note to avoid the spiny cactus plants that lay in wait at the edge of the road. Their razor-sharp edges were eager to cut into our flesh. Orange trees dotted the landscape as far as the eye could see. The dust rose in minute clouds as hooves struck the thirsty dirt. We pushed our way along the thousand-year-old donkey trail, rocking in the saddles as the sizzling sun scorched the brim of our sombreros. We perspired profusely in the arid heat. We kept moving, creating a slight artificial breeze as the movement of our horses cut through the hot, still air of midday.

My reprieve from Romero's antics was short-lived as we began to descend into a valley. Romero started to pick up the pace in response to the natural gravitational pull of the downward trail. This was his calculated opportunity to rid himself of the rider on his back. He pulled the reins from my hands, tucked his head between his front legs, and began pitching and bucking as we rolled down the hill in a most precarious manner. I hung on and leaned backward, trying to regain control as I rode him out until we once again met level ground. This would be the predictable trademark of future rides with Romero when the stakes would be much higher. As the elevation of the trail increased, so did the gravity of danger.

Our introductory ride had been a short jaunt, and we returned to the stables just below the villa. We relaxed in the luscious gardens that surrounded the tranquil blue waters of the pool as we waited the call to dinner.

I was being initiated into the culture of the Old World, where dining is a very social event not measured in minutes but hours. It was a multicourse meal, as one delectable culinary delight was brought out at a time. We chatted and formed friendships that would endure long after the holiday as the plates were cleared. We soon retired to the game room and milled around the pool table. Everyone was engaged in conversation as we toasted our hosts with the sweet sips of aperitifs.

Morning dawned early as we met at the stables to begin the first leg of our week-long ride. The grooms had the horses tacked up as many of the older riders took to the mounting blocks. I sprung up in the stirrup and settled into the saddle. I quickly swung my left leg forward while retrieving one of the billets from under the flap of the saddle. I checked the tightness of my girth, not leaving anything to chance. Satisfied that all was safe, I returned my leg into its rightful position. I was prepared for the game to begin as I noted with caution the mischievous glint in Romero's wild eye.

In the first few days of our adventure, one of the guest riders decided to keep count in his vacation journal of Romero's attempts to buck me off. I was suspicious that there was even a betting pool created for this unceremonious sport of dumping the rider, myself being the object of the bets. By the end of our ride, the score tallied twenty-eight attempts, but thankfully, none were successful. I told everyone that I was too scared to come off, especially when some of the drops were close to 1,000 feet. I couldn't imagine dying in a gorge, my fate sealed as a result of an ill-mannered horse in a foreign land an ocean and continent away.

Every day, we climbed higher and higher, making switchbacks as we rode. We averaged seven hours in the saddle each day, standing in the stirrups for the majority of the ride as we freed the horses' hindquarters. They lifted us up over the mountains with each straining push forward. We rested for lunch in small villages where the local canteens provided food and beer for drink. The beer was probably safer for foreigners to drink than the local water. At least most of the riders appreciated the beer. With our appetites satisfied, we soon mounted up and continued to the next destination. With repetition, we followed the foot-wide paths of dust, cactus, and rock.

The scenery was breathtaking, but it was dangerous, too, as loose rock often broke away beneath our horses' hooves as they scrambled to climb the hills. As the trail rounded a wide bend at one point in the ride, we were paired and put to the gallop along a dried-up riverbed. The horses knew the route all too well and weren't about to be dictated to as to speed or direction. We flew across the gravel rock at breakneck speed, unable to control our mounts. The horses grabbed the bits between their teeth and leaned into the bridle as we stood in the stirrups and leaned backward in protest. Following the riverbed, the horses finally slid their haunches to a sudden halt as a sheer wall of rock closed their path. Most of the riders had utter terror in their eyes as their pale skin reflected the fear that tormented them on this dash down the trail. By the grace of God, Mother Nature saved them with her wall of stone.

At least the rides continued to be entertaining for the rest of the group, as I was challenged on a daily basis to sit deep, tight, and survive. The day trips were eventful and full of intrigue. One evening, we rode late into the darkness of nightfall. We were negotiating down a stubborn mountain path and preparing to enter a village that rested at the foothills. It was so dark that we couldn't see our hands in front of our faces and could only listen to the horses' hooves as they picked their way along in the blackness of the night. Not a word was spoken as we swayed tiredly in our saddles, praying for the conclusion of the ride. Our mounts were masterful horses and very tractable. Still, one slip could spell disaster. Then it happened!

Travelling head to tail, one horse lost its footing and tumbled down the rocky path. The horse managed to recover and stood patiently for its rider to retrieve him. The rider wasn't so lucky. Blood streamed down his face, evidence of a nasty gash to his scalp. He moaned in pain. He had landed on a protruding rock that grazed his head and disturbed his level of consciousness. Sporting a makeshift dressing from his own shirt, he staggered to remount as we continued our journey down the mountain. We arrived in the village a short time later. The town had no doctor. There was only a local veterinarian of sorts who cleaned the wound and dressed it. The rider would have to take a few days off from the tour in order to recover from his injuries and a possible concussion. The next morning, the silent grooms handed us our mounts, and we rode off minus one rider.

The daily rides would take us through the breeding pastures of the famous fighting bulls of Spain. There were no fences separating us from them. When approaching a herd of grazing matador killers, we were instructed to be silent and walk slowly in a single file. We weren't to draw attention to ourselves or our horses. That could give the bulls an excuse to test their courage. It was a nerve-racking, ten-minute stroll through the pasture of the bulls, but we made it safely through.

Rail service was scattered indiscriminately throughout the area. As we dutifully followed Antonio, a large freight train chugged behind us, parallel to our path. Antonio pulled his horse up and encouraged the rest of us to follow him as he raised his arm and circled the air in a forward motion.

As the train approached, Antonio's direction took on more urgency as he shouted down the line. The only problem was that he spoke in Spanish. Since Romero had been a spoiler, he had been relegated to the back of the group. We were outcasts trailing the group at some distance. I wasn't sure if Antonio wanted me to stay put or gallop up. I could hear the blow of the train's whistle that mocked Antonio's frustrated commands as it drowned out the last few words he uttered. I decided to stay put and calm my horse. My mind quickly reminded me of the boy who perished at home when his horse panicked and ran into a train at a level crossing years ago. I turned Romero's head away from the fast-approaching locomotive. Luckily for me, my instincts were right, and I had made the right decision. Although excitedly prancing on the spot, Romero heeded my pleas to stay as the train roared by us. This was no time for Romero to be playing his "buck the rider off" game. As the clicking on the rails trailed off in the distance and the flashes of boxcars gave way to reveal my riding companions, I quickly regrouped with the other riders, much to everyone's relief.

At one point in our journey, we all clambered into a bus to visit the ancient town of Alora. The horses were ponied to the next destination. It was a day out of the saddle, allowing us to become tourists for a day while visiting the shops and making those souvenir purchases. Our accommodations were in a beautiful hotel at the edge of town. I tried speaking my limited Spanish, asking for my room number. The clerk smiled and said in English, "Very good, *señorita.*" I felt foolish and returned the smile with a hint of embarrassment.

A group of us decided to visit a local bar that evening. We had been advised of a curfew, which was part of the town's bylaw. A young German in our group of riders named Helmut befriended me. We talked for most of the evening until a brazen young Spaniard asked me for a dance. It was a slow dance, and I can remember the fellow holding me so tightly that I could hardly breathe. I didn't like it and returned to the table as the music faded away. I sought the comfort and friendship of Helmut as he escorted me out of the bar with the rest of our group and the security of numbers it brought.

None of us had checked our timepieces. It was after midnight, and the curfew was in effect. We noticed headlights of a car approaching from an intersecting street. We dove into some bushes to conceal our presence. The car drove slowly by as we held our breath and crouched in silence. The handheld light from a police patrol car beamed along the alleyways. The last thing we wanted was to end up in a Spanish jail without our passports!

With the danger passed, we hastily beat a path to the hotel, giggling like schoolkids all the way. When we approached the hotel, we discovered that the front doors were locked. Now what? We huddled together for a quick game plan. Helmut contemplated our situation and decided that the best course of action would be to attract some attention to our plight. He picked up a tiny pebble and threw it at one of the first-floor windows that cast a light out across the yard. It worked. The night watchman opened the window as we pleaded with him to let us in. A few moments later, he appeared at the front door. We quietly stole humbly away to our rooms.

In the morning, a bus waited to drive us to our next rendezvous with the horses. En route, we stopped for a brief rest so that we could all stretch our legs and find some comfort stations. It was a quaint little village at the bottom of a mountain. A young boy walked by leading a small donkey laden with an incredible load of wood. How strong this little hairy donkey was. I could truly appreciate the phrase "beast of burden."

Our interpreter signalled us to the bus as she started the head count. We were missing one person. A search party was formed as we fanned out in groups of two, looking and calling for our wayward member. This was gypsy territory and noted for bands of robbers. After an hour of walking the streets and dirt paths, the missing person was located. Local authorities had found her walking down a road. She had taken a wrong turn and lost her way. Back in the safety of numbers, we clambered into the bus and continued on to our destination.

We rode off on the final leg of our trip in the mountains. We climbed to an elevation where the air became chilly and the oxygen levels were depleted to some degree. It was nightfall when we arrived in the village. We dismounted and entered through two large doors with our horses in tow. The doors led into a house as we crossed a short hall and out to a courtyard where the stables were. We handed over our mounts to the now familiar grooms and were shown to our rooms for the evening. It seemed like walking horses through someone's house was a rather bizarre arrangement.

After dinner, I joined up with an English mother and daughter duo. The mother introduced me to the amber glow of sherry, saying it would take the chill out of my bones. *Strong stuff,* I thought as I slowly sipped from the sherry glass. It did the trick as far as warming me or at least giving the illusion of warmth. In the morning, we would be bussed back to the villa to say our goodbyes.

Romero had taken me to the brink of death at times with his vaulting lifts from behind. We had travelled at speed down a hair's breadth path at the edge of a cliff. He had made me a better, more cautious rider and taught me survival skills on horseback that I would never forget.

I ambled down to the stable one last time before I took my leave for the airport. Romero stood quietly in his stall, munching away at the sun-bleached, straw-coloured hay. He lifted his head for a few moments, grinding the scratchy hay between his molars. His eyes teased me with a mischievous grin as if to say, "Catch you next time, partner." I patted him on the neck and told him to be kinder to his next rider. They might not want to play his game.

The plane lifted off, heading north to the city of Madrid. For the next few days, I played tourist before boarding a plane for home. It would be a cultural experience and a fantastic finale to my vacation of a lifetime. How would I know there would be another vacation of a lifetime to come years later?

Chapter 8

Building the Dream

I was reaching my early twenties and had met a wonderful man I fell head over heels for. He wasn't a horse person but showed an interest in my passion. He was from Chicago, and I was ready to take the plunge and move to the United States to follow my heart. I had to sell my beloved Mags and Whisper. It was a very sad day when the trailer arrived to take them to their new owners. Still, I didn't want to be like the poor lad who lost his pony Pat to another world. I wished my horses a good life with their new owners. I was growing up and had to make hard decisions for my future. Sadly, the courtship ended painfully, and I would be horseless again for a few years.

The year 1973 brought me back into horse ownership with the purchase of a weanling Morgan stud colt. I had met the man who would share my dream and who would encourage me. He would often tease me, telling everyone that he had financed part of my first horse venture into purebred stock.

In 1978, I took on a new role as a wife. Together, Robert and I would tackle the challenges that lay ahead of us in all the twists and turns life threw at us. We moved into a small, one-bedroom apartment. Neither of us had ever experienced apartment living. I felt estranged from my country life. Even suburbia was better than this. My horse kept me occupied when I came home from a long, boring day sitting at a desk and then boarding a train for the long trip home. It was a welcomed change to pull on a pair of jeans and drive to the stable with renewed vigour. As my husband worked shifts, often the nights in the apartment were lonely and sometimes frightening. There were occasional altercations between neighbouring residents that spilled out into the hallway outside our apartment door. My only protection was a boisterous cockatiel named Cheeky who screamed her objections from the safety of her wire cage. Then there was our late-night Saturday entertainment. As we lay in bed, we listened to the *squeak, squeak* and then the lion's roar from the floor above as we giggled and huddled beneath the sheets. If that bed had casters, I'm sure it would have kept us up all night with the roll and pitch of the lovers' wave of amorous intensity.

Six months into our lease, we mutually agreed that it was time to move on. We broke out of the renter's world and purchased a small bungalow. It was a stone's throw from the converted cow barn we were renting at the time.

Prior to our marriage, we purchased a brand-new motor home. As we drove the cottage on wheels off the lot, our parents thought it was a frivolous and foolish idea. While we owned the moving motel, we enjoyed two wonderful vacations and an affordable, romantic honeymoon that took us to the eastern shores of the Atlantic. That motorized home on wheels translated into a hefty down payment on our first home. The insane investment turned out to be a blessing. We sold the coach for the same amount of money as the purchase price.

We settled into life as homeowners for the first time, and we were happy in our own dwelling. The stable was only minutes away, and life seemed perfect.

A few years after moving into our home, we received an unsettling phone call. Through a Chinese translator, the caller identified himself as the new owner of the farm property we were renting for our horses. The stable and property had been sold without us being notified. Month after month, the rent increases came. It was no longer feasible for us to remain with so many repairs needed to the building and fences. The owner wasn't interested in maintaining the property, as it was only an investment property to him. Although our future plans included looking for a farm of our own, the timetable had been pushed ahead with this recent change in landlords. Mortgage rates were at an unprecedented high level. It certainly was not a buyer's market.

Finding what we needed and what we could afford was a painstaking experience. By this time, we had registered our farm prefix, and a permanent location was in the cards. It was such a frustrating process as we walked the floors of many houses and stables. Either the dwelling was marginal at best or the reverse. Prices were outlandish and unattainable as we wearily stepped from the car to the gravel driveway of countless properties pegged with For Sale signs.

Winter was closing in as we drove to a quaint little village east of Oshawa. The roadmap took us directly to a pretty parcel of land with forestlands embracing the pastures of the 25-acre lot. An old farmhouse stood tall and stately amid the clutter of fall leaves blanketing the ground in various stages of decay. The only structures on the property were a dilapidated hip roof barn to the north-west of the property and an open, run-in shed to the south. No hay had been baled from the cleared land in years, and the fences were rusty page wire. Still, the beauty of the landscape and its location to good roads and easy access to major routes was ideal. The price was more than we could ever afford, so we reluctantly made an offer substantially below the market listing. We left the rest up to fate, believing that if it was to be, so be it.

By early evening, the telephone rang, and the news was delivered. Our offer had been accepted! Closing was near Christmas, so the bulk of the move would have to wait until spring.

As newly weds, we were now solely responsible for all financial matters relating to home ownership and the demands of rural life. We felt the financial sting of the welcome wagon to country living. No longer were we cushioned from the lower hydro rates of city dwellers as we realized a tripled cost in electricity. Every repair that needed doing, regardless of the relatively small size, started in the thousands of dollars, not hundreds. The antique oil furnace chewed up any savings we had been accustomed to with the high efficiency gas furnace in our previous house. And then there was the well drilling and new septic system the following spring. We survived a backed-up septic system that lay dormant in the frozen, snow-covered ground. We searched in vain for the vent pipe one late night in February as the temperatures fell well below the freezing mark. Then there was the upgrade to the house with vinyl siding to deter some of the winter bite from blowing through the many cracks in our century-old home. Still, the sunsets were a glorious painter's palette, and the cheery welcome to dawn with the birds welcoming spring soothed our misgivings.

We had settled into country life and began the lifelong challenges of completing our blueprint for a sustainable and comfortable horse farm. The hardships lay ahead, so with age in our favour, we slowly started to build our dream.

We were denied a family of the conventional style. Although disheartened by the fact that raising children was not to be, looking back, I'm comforted by the thought that the All Mighty had a plan for me all along. Devoting my talents to the equine species has enriched my life. It was a gift I had been given and a dream I had to follow. And so the children of our house had more than two legs and came in a variety of species not exclusive to horses.

For the first time, I could offer training, boarding, and enhance my small breeding herd of Morgan horses on my own property. It was the beginning of my base of clientele with loyal customers that would return over the decades.

I looked forward to each spring being rewarded with my breeding attempts the year before. I never tire of hearing the soft nicker of a newborn foal as it struggles to its feet. There is something mystical about the whole event that softens the heart and puts life into perspective.

After several years of breeding, my horses were ready for the open market. Selling the first couple of horses was hard. I was there when they foaled and fitted them with their first halters. I had trained them and now had to let them go. Our breeding operation expanded, and so did the training. My life was full.

Like most horse operations, the proprietors hold other jobs outside the farm. My days began at 4:00 a.m., doing chores in the stable and turning horses out before washing up and changing clothes. As the car rolled in the driveway somewhere around 5:30 in the evening, I brought the horses in from the fields. I broke open bales of sweet hay and distributed equal portions to the long line of box stalls. Next, I brought out the grain buckets as the horses called excitedly for the molasses-dressed feed.

By early evening, I started the training routine after finishing up a hurried evening meal. By nine o'clock, the last stall door was latched and the lights switched to darkness as I turned and walked up the short pathway to the house. The scenario was repeated for twenty-two years, 365 days a year.

The word *vacation* never enters our vocabulary. Farmers don't take time off for vacations. Choosing to live with horses or farm animals of any kind is a lifestyle alteration. Time off from your offsite job is spent on farm maintenance. There is always something that needs fixing.

As we grew in stalls and business, we had considered building an indoor arena. Still, the sticker price for such an undertaking matched the mortgage on the house. The wish list just kept being pushed ahead to the future. That would soon change after an unfortunate winter ride in the forest.

On a clear, sunny Sunday afternoon in early January, I saddled up my lovely palomino mare, Trillium Justina. I was looking forward to a relaxing ride in the forest. The big mare quietly ambled her way through the dense, snow-covered brush. The soft fallen snow that had cascaded down from the sky the previous night muted her hoof beats. The path opened up to the service road leading to the seedling beds of the provincial forest station. I pressed the rein on the side of her neck and nudged her to the right as we proceeded onto the road.

It was a beautiful day; it was not too cold, and it was bright and oh so quiet. It was a nice hack as I rode slowly, waiting for a client boarder back at the stable to tack up and meet me on the trail. I turned at the fork in the road and headed west down the familiar trail. The snow crystals sparkled like a million diamonds. The air was refreshing as I took a deep breath and settled my hips down into the broad leather of the Western saddle. Justina swung her head in the rhythm of the gait. She was relaxed and enjoying the serenity of the woods.

We rounded a small bend in the trail, and as we started to straighten to the lean of the path, disaster struck! The scene played out in slow motion in my head as I recall crashing to the ground.

Justina suddenly fell sideways as her bare hooves shot out from beneath her. She went down hard, pinning my leg beneath her. A thin dusting of snow hid the glassy ice that filled a depression in the earth. The ice was unforgiving as the horse thrashed about and fell several more times, narrowly missing my bruised body. She eventually scrambled to a firm patch of ground and picked herself up. The reins hung over her head as she stood patiently waiting for my return. I got on my knees and pulled myself up onto the same frozen grass that she had used to exit from the ice. I attempted to stand and quickly found myself lying on the ground. My leg was twisted in an awkward and unusual position. It was broken. I heard the grinding sound of the fractured tibia. It was held only by skin, muscle, and tendon. I lay quietly for a moment, deciding what I should do. I was about a quarter of a mile from the stable. At least the sun was warm and the air still. The horse stayed with me, curiously dropping her nose to inspect my broken body. I was banking on my horse boarder taking the same fork in the road and come upon me for my deliverance. I didn't want to succumb to hypothermia, so I decided that I could at least start the trek back, pulling myself through the snow by using my arms and elbows.

It was probably ten minutes later that I began to call out for help. I had only managed about 50 feet when the rider appeared on his little Arabian gelding. He offered to put me on his horse and take me back. By this time, the numbness had subsided, and the pain was searing. Any thought of bumping along while lying over a horse's back with my fractured leg dangling was simply out of the question. I sent him back to bring my husband.

Twenty minutes passed as I lay writhing in pain. I stopped crawling through the snowdrifts, knowing that help would be forthcoming at any moment. Bob had to go to the forest keeper's house to get the gate key so he could drive the car in from the road. Finally, I heard the dull rumble of a car approaching. Bob had solicited the help of another boarder who just happened to be a volunteer firefighter with first aid training. They carefully lifted me into the backseat of the car. My leg was sandwiched between two pillows as they drove me to the nearby hospital.

Justina made her own way home and was untacked while I lay in the emergency room of the local hospital. The break was so severe that the emergency room doctor sent me by ambulance to another hospital in a nearby city. There, a top orthopaedic surgeon could review my injuries and assess appropriate treatment. I was loaded up on pain-killing Demerol for the trip out. Fortunately, I was spared surgery, as the break was clean without any splinters. The surgeon wanted to work with it in a cast. Eventually, I would be weaned to a brace.

Just a few days after the cast had been set, I returned to the hospital in excruciating pain. The cast had to be cut open to relieve the pressure from the swelling screaming to be free of the plaster. The next several months were the most difficult. Sleeping in a reclining chair is not the most comfortable option, but the only one at the time. The barn chores were doled out to everyone and anyone that offered their help.

As the days passed, I became more and more restless. Boredom sadistically crept in and took hold. I wanted so badly to go to the barn. When I was stable enough, I was driven down to the barn, and I walked in on my crutches. It was good to be back as the familiar scent of the stable filled my lungs. The sweet smell of hay and even the whiff of ammonia was like heaven.

When spring finally came, I knew that I needed to get back on the horse. I was still healing in a brace when I asked the doctor if I could sit on the horse. Owning horses himself, he knew all too well the stubbornness of emotional attachment to the horse. He also knew the mental challenge one faces after a severe riding mishap. He reluctantly agreed to my request, but only if several people headed the horse and spotted for me.

I managed to swing the cumbersome right leg over the horse. It was good to be in the saddle again. I asked to be led around the small, round ring. I accomplished three laps of the ring before the pain became unbearable. Still, I was happy that I had gotten back on if only as a confidence builder. I didn't fear the horse, as I knew the circumstances were beyond anyone's control. It was purely an accident absent of malice.

It was almost a year before I resumed full use of the leg and accompanying strength. Months of physical therapy helped return me to the saddle. Outdoor winter riding would no longer be an activity I would participate in. Those days were over. It was then that we decided it was time to include an indoor arena in our horse facility.

We investigated potential builders. We thought we had done a thorough job before making the financial plunge into building our riding arena. The farm was just about paid off, and with the erection of an arena, it put us back in a financial drain once again. Mammoth projects such as these, never seems to go entirely smoothly. Ours was no exception. Between building permits, contractors, subcontractors, and months of construction, the arena finally came to fruition. We looked with pride on our lovely yellow arena that would protect us from what wickedness Mother Nature might dish up. We looked forward to our first winter with utter confidence.

As the temperatures dropped and the frost drove deeper and deeper into the ground, we listened curiously to the odd twang of the guy wires that connected the walls to prevent them from shifting. By mid-February, the building was stressed so much that sixty-four skylights that ran the perimeter of the building just below the roofline cracked and broke. The steel wall beneath them buckled and twisted with the heaving of frost. It was like an earthquake had struck our brand-new arena.

My heart sank as every day I walked down to the stable bearing witness to the grotesque twist of steel and fibreglass. It was only months before that it stood firm and bright in the morning sun. I was so near to tears as I heard the pop of another fracturing skylight ricochet off the metal wall. It would take a couple of years and several thousands of dollars in repair and engineer and lawyers' fees, excluding all the inconvenience and loss of use, before it was right again. We only recovered about half of the total expenses through an out-of-court settlement and had to swallow the rest. We saved where we could, but our spanking-new building had been so damaged that it appeared old before its time.

Chapter 9

A Colt for the Gelding

As the years passed and with Samson, our leading stallion, now sprouting the occasional white hair above his eyes, Father Time reminded me that I should consider my options for a future sire. Being particular in finding the most agreeable temperament and conformation that would complement Sam's best attributes would be a long journey. With each year of foals, several colts that held promise of walking in their father's shadow didn't measure up to the standards I had chosen as they matured. One colt in particular seemed to have the grace and look of a champion that might well have the making for my next stallion to carry on the lineage. He was quick to learn, sassy, and full of inner confidence. By his second birthday, he was firmly testing the waters of obedience and respect. Playful by nature, it was difficult to deter him from the dangerous game of touch. He delighted in rising up on his hind legs as he reached to catch a shoulder. Reprimanding him every time with the sting of a whip didn't do much to dissuade him from his antics.

One afternoon, I was leading him into his stall, being mindful of his foolish pranks as he tossed his mane in the air and pranced along the concrete aisle. A tug on the end of the shank kept him somewhat focused and agreeable. With my back to the doorway, I stood at his side and quietly lifted the crown piece of his halter over his ears, taking every measure of precaution. In a micron of a second, I lay bleeding on floor of his stall. My cheek had a gaping gash, while the top of my head throbbed with pain. The colt had reeled around as if propelled with rocket fuel. With precision, he lifted with such swiftness that I never saw the hooves that crashed into my head and face. He knocked me down hard into the bed of freshly laid pine shavings.

Bleeding profusely, my fingers swept the immediate space around me as I sifted through the bedding in search of my twisted wire frames. Latching onto the glasses, I fumbled to put them on. The lower bottom of the frame was now resting in the newly formed crater of my left cheek. I stumbled to my feet as the colt stood standing at the back of his stall. He was trembling with fear of retribution. He must have realized the seriousness of his actions and the punishment that was sure to ensue. I steadied myself by leaning against the wood plank wall. Staggering out of the dull grey light of the stall, I managed to latch the door and secure it.

Dazed and staggering as if a loitering drunkard trying to navigate his way home, I struggled toward the office. Each step was imprinted with a trail of blood trickling behind me. Realizing my injuries were potentially serious, I reached for the phone on the desk. A river of blood now flowed down my face, still not stemmed by the clotting process. I rushed to press the keypad of the phone with my index finger as I attempted to dial 911. My vision was so impaired by the blood and trauma to my head that I couldn't see the numbers. I guessed their placement. Each time I attempted to depress the three simple digits, an annoying recorded message played on the receiver, saying, "Please check the number and try your call again." I took a deep breath and made a deliberate effort to hit the correct keys firmly and accurately. Finally, I connected, and an operator came on the line.

My first aid training came to the forefront as if shaken from the conscientiousness of my memory. I relayed my injuries and location as calmly and definitively as I could to the emergency responder. I was adamant that the ambulance was to come to the stable area rather than the house. I returned the receiver to its cradle and walked the short distance to the refrigerator by the main doors of the stable. My legs were shaking as I reached for the freezer compartment to retrieve a couple of ice packs reserved for lameness and injuries of the horse. My still quivering legs carried me back to the office where I opened the linen cupboard and grabbed a somewhat clean towel from the shelf. Slowly, I turned my attention toward the bench in the main aisle where I settled into respite with my lacerations. One ice pack rested on the top of my head, and another pack wrapped in the towel pressed against my cheek. Both hands were occupied as I sat and waited.

The barn was quiet and asleep in the late morning sun as I listened for the whining call of an ambulance approaching. Time seemed to pass agonizingly slowly. Finally, the faint cry of the ambulance began to increase in volume as it approached from the south. I listened anxiously as the wail of the siren began to fade. The driver had driven past the stable lane, instead directing his vehicle toward the house. *Figures,* I thought. A few moments later, the rumble of the ambulance's engine came to a halt outside the main entrance to the stable. As the doors of the ambulance swung opened, my panicked nerves eased.

After the paramedics quickly evaluated me, they helped me into the ambulance and on to a waiting stretcher. The vehicle was put into gear, and we rode south-west toward the hospital. It would be a mercifully short but bumpy ride.

The attendants monitored my vitals and talked to me while en route. Surveying my state of functioning mind and mental faculties, they tested me and subjected me to the usual barrage of questions, such as my name, date of birth, and so on. Everything jingled and swung to the roll of the ambulance as I lay in an unnatural pose, staring upward at concerned faces. This would be my second ride in a hospital on wheels. It was a trip I hadn't envisioned and didn't care to repeat. Within moments of arriving at the hospital, I started to feel very ill and lapsed out of consciousness. I remember the oxygen mask covering my face as I regained a more realistic level of awareness of my surroundings. The urgent need to vomit subsided.

The afternoon passed painfully slowly (no pun intended) as I lay in the sterile white of the emergency ward. I had been wheeled into the radiology department for some panoramic pictures of my skull. I didn't feel very comfortable trying to maintain my equilibrium while balancing on a tottery stool without benefit of the reassuring arm of a nurse to hold on to. I managed.

The numerous floaters in my eyes that had plagued my vision were now gone. It is amazing what a good knock on the head can do to dissolve these annoying vision intruders.

I must have been starting to feel more humanlike, as the pains of hunger were pleading with me to satisfy them. Since any form of food was forbidden at this point during my medical observation, I began to wonder about the deep gash that still required attention. The remnants of stable debris stuck stubbornly to the thick, oozing blood of the wound. I worried that the time elapsed might make the repair process more difficult. From dealing with horse injuries, I knew the window of time was relatively short if sutures were required to close the wound. Drying of the skin tissues would be detrimental. At long last, a surgical team came to clean up my altered appearance. By now, deep swelling and bruising had settled in. Despite the cooling agents of chopped ice that rested over my left eye and cheek, it hadn't retarded the advances of the ballooning effect.

The cut was irrigated with a saline solution and meticulously cleaned as they applied a layer of glue to seal my cheek. I was relieved that catgut wasn't employed for this repair. Numbed by the blow, my cheek and teeth felt like they had received a good dose of dental freezing. As the doctors and nurses filed past my bedside on their rounds, they exchanged comments as to the awful shiner I sported over my left eye. By then, my eye was totally squeezed shut with unrelenting swelling. Some remarks were obviously sympathetic to my plight. Others made comments with a not-so-subtle humour. Somehow, I didn't find it very amusing.

Satisfied that I was stable enough to leave the hospital, I was released into the care of my husband. My short stay had prompted a new name for me with the hospital staff. I would be named, "Lady Kicked in Head by Horse." On subsequent visits to the emergency department, the staff referred to me by that nickname. It seems that from then on, if I ever enter the ER again at that hospital, they will simply write on my chart, "Lady Kicked in Head by Horse." I must have made quite the impression.

Still uneasy in gait, I walked through the corridor, nearly crashing into the clear wall and glass doors that led to the exit. The only good thing I could look forward to was food. The pounding headache began to fade as I eased myself into a chair at our favourite Friday night dining haunt.

There we sat as people glanced over at the strange dinner table foursome. I really didn't care what people thought; I was so hungry that the disfigurement of my face was the least of my immediate priorities. I wasn't prepared to repeat my explanation of what happened to so many curious folks. Instead, I let them fantasize. I'm sure my husband must have been categorized as the suspect in this matter while suspicious eyes glanced over at our little dinner party gathering.

Across from the table spread with a vinyl cloth and scattered with menus sat my friend and veterinarian. His useless arm rested in the pale yellow sling of hospital issue. His shoulder had been torn from its socket by an ornery cow a day before. The once displaced shoulder screamed with pain, but less so since it was manipulated back into its proper housing by a team of doctors. As our hot, steamy dinner plates were lowered strategically in front of us, Harry slipped his arm cautiously from its tethered nest and prepared to take up his utensils. We must have appeared like a couple of fierce pit bulls salivating over our daily meal after doing battle. By the look of things, we must have been champions of the defeated.

I determined that my right jaw would do all chewing as I gingerly opened my mouth with trepidation. At last, a small morsel of food passed my lips. Aw, what a triumph!

As the dinner hour progressed, Harry and I compared notes and agreed not to tell anyone our occupations while we were in this early state of repair. We discussed a date to surgically end the offending colt's behaviour. As soon as both of us healed sufficiently to operate, the scalpel would put an end to the colt's little game of touch.

The day had come when revenge would be mine as I stood at the tranquilized colt's head, my face still colourful and swollen as the freezing was administered. The vet attended to the castration process, his injured arm held close to his side. The deed was done. Harry said, "I hope he doesn't hold a grudge."

In the following months, I underwent more visits to the radiology department for frontal face bone images. I required rounds of dental work to secure my damaged teeth through root canal surgeries. Slowly, the feeling started to creep back into the left side of my face as the nerves began to regenerate. Daily applications of Vitamin E cream and facial massage hastened the healing process until only a very faint trace of scarring remained. The redness lessened, and the swelling over my eye retreated, along with the colourful rainbow that surrounded it. It would be the better part of six months before I was fully restored.

Today, anyone handling stallions at the farm is required to wear helmets and lead with a stallion chain. It is a precautionary exercise that was initiated by one playful colt that is now an adorable, sweet gelding. This once naughty colt has since had stellar performances in the show arena, awarding him several championships.

Chapter 10

On the Road

Upon reflection, life behind the wheel hauling horse trailers can be very interesting. Our many miles of travel with horses have been punctuated with near disasters and insufferable inconveniences. With the St Christopher medal riding in my husband's back pocket, heavenly intervention has spared us much grief. It has also blessed us with a good dose of luck.

Our first horse trailer was an old English built box called a Rice trailer. It was unique in its day with the British design of a front offload. It was spacious and heavily built. It would be the trailer my young stallion would call home while travelling the high roads to horse shows, parades, and breed demonstrations. Foxy loved the ride of the roomy trailer even when it pushed us through a red light en route to a horse show. The weight of this trailer with its ancient mechanical braking system wasn't all that efficient and perhaps lethal. Luckily, no other traffic was involved when we screeched to a halt in the middle of the intersection. Foxy relaxed his stance, and we continued our travel. We were mindful to allow more stopping distance for traffic lights after that incident.

On one trip east, a tire blew on the trailer, and we limped to the side of the road. The tire iron proved useless, as the bolts that held the wheel in place had been welded. No amount of superhuman strength was going to budge those wheel nuts. To add to our trouble, we discovered that they were an odd metric size, as well. Of course, this was before the instatement of the metric system in Canada.

Travelling on the shoulder of the highway, we took the first exit ramp and pulled into a small garage. It took some doing, but the mechanic on duty finally extracted the wheel from the trailer. After searching through an enormous mountain of used tires, he found an odd size, although it was bald. It fit! Three hours later, we pulled out of the service station and continued eastward.

It was a long horse show, finishing up sometime around midnight. We walked Foxy up the ramp and closed the doors of the trailer behind him. Off we went, heading home.

The miles passed beneath the trailer as the traffic disappeared into the early hours of the morning. The fuel gauge indicated that we would soon be riding on fumes. We rolled off on every exit in search of a gas station that was open, but every one remained in darkness. Desperate not to be stranded on the side of the highway, we drove into a small, lonely gas bar. We curled up on the cots in the back of the van and tried to sleep. It was a restless retirement to the night as Foxy jiggled the trailer with his casual movements. He munched away for brief periods, pulling hay from the net that swung freely from the ring in the trailer. He was content enough and probably more so than his weary owners. Several hours after the sun rose, a car pulled in, and the driver opened the station. With a full tank of fuel, we urged the gas pedal to take us back on the highway. Home was our final destination.

The next day, we received a call from one of the owners at the stable who was somewhat concerned that Foxy had been lying in his stall for hours. There was nothing wrong with him. He was just as exhausted as we were from the horse show and trailering ordeal. Foxy loved his sleep and earned every minute of it. He was a tough competitor in the ring and a veteran traveller in his rolling box.

When it came time to trade up, we purchased a lovely new horse trailer with white interior. The exterior was painted a spiffy royal blue accented with white pinstripes. Foxy deserved a new home on wheels. Unfortunately, it was not a mutual acceptance on Foxy's part. He loved the old Rice trailer that had been his home for hundreds of miles. Although the new trailer was bright and inviting, Foxy walked up the ramp but soon became very claustrophobic. He scrambled and tried to lie down even before the trailer was in motion. Every time we loaded him, the symptoms and reaction became more pronounced as he struggled in panic. We were stymied. It wasn't an option to bring back his old trailer, as it had been sold. Still, we feared that if we couldn't resolve the problem with the new trailer, his showing days would be over. So we experimented.

We removed the full partition that divided the trailer. Foxy seemed to relax and eventually travelled calmly. When we showed our broodmare, Foxy would have to share his trailer space with his mate. We decided to place a simple bar down the centre of the trailer with no other divider other than the bar separating him from the mare. It worked. Both horses travelled well, securing their balance with open space. We dressed them in bell boots and leg wraps as protection in case of accidental treading. For years, Foxy and Ginger loaded and hauled in complete comfort.

As time passed and our farm grew, we opted for an even larger trailer. We purchased a new, six-horse van that was well constructed. Now with the considerably larger trailer and heavier load capacity, we traded our half-ton pickup for a one-ton heavy dually. We soon learned not to believe the manufacture load capacity ratings after serious breakdowns. In five years, we went through four engines. Even with engine enhancements, such as a turbo charger, extra capacity radiators, and oil coolers, we still suffered breakdowns. Some hills were unmerciful as the truck dropped lower and lower, managing a speed of 10 miles per hour or less. I could have walked beside the truck. We rocked in our seats, motioning the truck forward with every minute drop in speed.

On one occasion, we were heading home after a horse show in darkness with six horses in the van. My husband hadn't topped up the tank when we left for the show, and we were running on fumes. The engine cut out, and we rolled to the side of the road. It was close to midnight, and the road was desolate and very black. We couldn't see our hands in front of our faces, and it was eerily quiet. We managed to call another Morgan horse breeder who lived about fifteen minutes away. He kindly pulled himself away from his warm bed and hooked up his horse van. He came to our rescue.

The horses were transferred from our trailer to his with only the headlights and four-way flashers from the vehicles warning other approaching traffic that might find its way to our location. With the horses all safely loaded, our Good Samaritan took our horses to his farm. He put some of his own horses out in pasture and gave our horses stalls for the night. In due time, our disabled truck was towed and put back into service. The moral of this story: don't ever let a diesel engine fuel tank run dry!

On one haul, we blew the engine shortly after coming onto a major highway. We rolled along on the shoulder of the road until we reached the first exit. We made it home travelling with flashers on at 10 miles per hour. That was the last time we hauled with that truck.

Big Blue, a medium-duty truck, was our next purchase. With more than twenty-five years of service, this vehicle has never failed us. It has handled our loads without complaint.

...

We have made several trips across the border, picking up horses we have purchased and delivering horses we have sold. It just seemed to be our luck that we managed to find construction zones in the various states in which we have travelled. It is ongoing, and we have yet to make a trip that was smooth sailing. We have encountered horrific thunderstorms with tornadolike winds when pushing through the black sky plains of Kansas at nightfall or manoeuvring the mountainous climbs of Wyoming en route to Utah. We met blinding fog, snow, and ice while crossing a long bridge from Vermont to New York. We had near misses with other vehicles that have lost control. But yet the most harrowing tale we can tell was when our Tilly almost splashed into the great St. Lawrence River while confined to her box in the trailer.

It had been a long day when we finally arrived at the border. Trillium Chantilly Lace had left home for a training sabbatical in New York, and we were bringing her home. We entered the customs inspection centre and backed our rig alongside the long row of idle, rattling tractor trailers. Tilly quietly munched on her hay as we made our way to the veterinary inspection area. With papers in hand, we patiently waited for the veterinarian to review our documentation. A voice from the sound system broke the monotone of the office paper shufflers pecking away at their keyboards as the wall clock slowly ticked off the minutes. "Owners of the blue horse trailer should return immediately to their vehicle." We didn't clue in that the blue horse trailer in question was ours. Suddenly, customs officers, truckers, and curious onlookers started running out the door. Bob followed in hot pursuit. I turned my head away from the veterinarian who was looking over my papers to see what all the commotion was about. I stopped breathing, and my eyes must have been popping out of my head. I flew through the door and ran toward our truck and trailer. In his fatigue, Bob had forgotten to put on the emergency brake. The truck doesn't have a park position, so it has to be left in neutral. As Tilly pawed impatiently in the trailer, the gentle rocking was enough to set the trailer in motion, and it was rolling backward. Concrete guards had been removed from the parking lot, so there was nothing to prevent vehicles from rolling off the end of the pavement. From there, it was a sheer drop some 30 feet to the rapidly flowing mighty St. Lawrence River below.

The trailer came to rest on its frame when the back wheels lost contact with the ground. Bob jumped into the truck as his foot heavily pressed against the brakes. The trailer dangled precariously over the edge of the parking lot. Everyone surveyed the dilemma. The veterinarian had followed me out the door. True to his profession, his immediate concern was for the horse trapped inside the trailer. His voice, threaded with anxious instruction, asked me to try to lead the horse off the trailer. "She's got to come off," he said. I knew it had to be done, but I was fearful for my own life, too. Should she panic and jump in the trailer, that might be all it would take to tip the scales and pull the whole rig down into the river below.

With trepidation, the right side ramp was gently lowered. The rear ramps were not an option, as they led out into thin air. Two-thirds of the side ramp was stabilized by the ground below. The last section of ramp had nothing under it for support. I cautiously walked into the horse van and quietly fastened a lead shank on to Tilly's halter. I acted as though nothing was wrong, and she remained calm and unaware of any danger. My worry was how she would react when she stepped on the ramp and saw nothing but air on her right side. I had to be the herd leader and have her follow me out without imparting to her any fear I might have. I took a deep breath, relaxed, and prayed to God to deliver us from this harm. I lowered the chest bar and walked nonchalantly beside Tilly. She strolled out of the trailer as if she were walking out of the barn on a lazy afternoon. There was a huge sigh of relief as I paraded her past the small, curious crowd that had gathered as I led her away from the truck and peril.

One of the truck drivers felt confident that his tractor could pull the rig forward. The macho, burly fellow from Quebec put on his grease-stained gloves and wrapped heavy link chains in place. The turbo kicked in as he dropped the tractor in gear. The trailer didn't budge. Upon closer inspection, it was found that the axles on the trailer were wedged against a steel culvert. It effectively prevented the trailer from moving ahead. If the tractor had been successful, the axles would have been ripped from the trailer, rendering it useless. A large tow truck was called. Minutes and then hours passed as I walked Tilly around the parking lot in endless circles. The forceful swishing sound of air brakes soon became a nonevent for Tilly. The pavement was unforgiving, and the heat was relentless. The constant smell of diesel spewing from the stacks of temporarily abandoned tractors made me nauseous as we paced back and forth. A customs officer asked if I would like to graze my horse at the side of the building. I thanked him, but since he couldn't tell me if the grass had been treated with herbicide, I declined his invitation with a courteous smile.

The heavy-duty tow truck finally arrived. The trailer frame had to be jacked up on blocks so the wheels could roll freely. A second tow truck was called in to help with the extraction. As the clock ticked by and several hundred dollars emptied from our pockets, the trailer finally rolled back onto the pavement, no worse for wear. We loaded Tilly, and we were given clearance to leave. It had been a humbling experience and one for the books, I'm sure. I think everyone was relieved that we were leaving. We later heard that the concrete barriers were put back in place after our little mishap.

Chapter 11

Living With a Fox

Foxy

For more than twenty-five years, a special horse shared his life with us. The passage of years brought with them many fond memories, along with the struggles and lessons he would teach us. In an abridged attempt, I hope to bring his story to life in the next few pages.

Lauralee Foxy Man was the first Morgan I had ever owned, or rather the first horse that owned me. He had become the realization of a dream and aspiration I had as a child to own one of his kind after reading about them in an all-breeds book. I loved all horses that had a mane and tail… even those without tails… and I still do. But there is something extraordinary, even magical, about the Morgan that still quickens the beat of my heart. Everything about the breed appealed to me as I turned the dog-eared pages of the library book. Even though I had never seen one in the flesh, I was hooked. I kept the mental image of the Morgan tucked away dormant for years until I met Foxy.

It all began when I saw a simple, large, bold sign bearing just two words—Morgan Horses—mounted above the sagging and creaking doors of an old wood-slat barn. Travelling at highway speed, the sign blurred as the car sped past it. The book I read so long ago tugged with spontaneity at the deep recesses of archival memories. The reawakened dreams from my early childhood urged me to turn back as I slowed the car and wheeled it around.

I gently pulled the steering wheel left as my car slowly rolled down the pothole-laden lane, stopping outside the dark grey, wooden bank barn. (I'm certain it had serviced more cows than horses in its day.) I was greeted upon my arrival and welcomed into the stable where I got my first look at a real live Morgan horse.

As I stepped into the subdued light of the converted staunches of a dairy barn, I was surprised that the horses looked so small. I had been used to horses of sixteen hands or larger, so when I saw the fourteen-hand (plus or minus) Morgan, I hated to admit that I was a little disappointed. It's amazing how one's impression can change when faced with reality. One by one, they were brought out for inspection as my earlier surprise at their size diminished.

The personalities and grandiose stances these diminutive horses had easily won me over. I was particularly impressed with the Morgan stallion, Cordon Marksman. The son of Bro-Rock March On by Vigilmarch seemed larger than life. My eyes critically gauged the form and structure of the horse. Everything fit well into this nice, tidy package. It was apparent that my initial faith in the breed was now reborn. I would have a Morgan at long last.

On my return visit to the breeder, I was led through a small walking gate that opened to a well-grazed summer pasture. The occasional long weed and thistle brushed my pant leg as we strolled farther into the pasture. We walked among the small herd of pregnant mares, some with foals at their sides. Interrupted by our presence only momentarily, they bent their heads low and continued to clip the sweet summer grass. Their muzzles massaged the next sheaths of grass ready for the picking as I surveyed them. A dark liver chestnut mare of good height raised her head as we approached. Her star prominently displayed between her soft brown eyes was like a target drawing me in. She was a maiden mare due to foal in the spring. With a critical eye, I stood back and looked for symmetry and balance. My eyes swept from the top of her ears, down her legs, across her back, and trailing off the hind leg. I repositioned myself directly in front of the mare. Finally, I walked to the back and studied the engine of the horse. I asked to see her move as I remained facing the hindquarters as her tail swished lazily from side to side, her belly heavy with foal. She travelled consistently with little deviation. Even though she had passed my physical requirements, her personality was just as important to me. After all, I wanted the whole package, not just good looks. The mare approached me with curiosity and promise. Her ears pricked nervously forward and back for a few moments until they settled in full expression and acceptance. *What a lovely mare,* I thought as she blew softly in my face with greetings of friendship. She cocked her head slightly to one side in recognition as I spoke to her.

Her name was Lauralee Delia Rose, and she was a daughter of Cordon Marksman, the stallion I had been introduced to on my earlier visit. Delia had been bred to a handsome young champion stallion of impeccable manners named Skipper Boy. How could I go wrong? I pulled out some money from my purse and made the commitment to purchase the mare's first foal.

In the wee early morning hours of May 12, 1973, just as daybreak was rising, a spunky colt squirmed his way into the world. He immediately made his presence known with a frantic whinny. His red chestnut coat glistened from its embryonic bath. Quickly, it dried and repelled the moisture as a tiny star fixed in the centre of his forehead became more visible. The star would later become the trademark that he would pass on to future generations.

I was informed of his arrival and the name the breeder had chosen for the colt. It didn't matter what gender the foal was as long as it was healthy. I can still remember as clearly as if I had stolen a time lapse from the past when I first peeked into the stall and gazed upon my perfect miniature Justin Morgan.

As I looked longingly at the little fellow who galloped around the stall with no inhibitions, the breeder approached me to explain how she had come up with the name of the foal. Using his pedigree as a means to finding a suitable name, she explained that she combined part of a name from both his dam and sire to come up with Foxy Man. The farm prefix was added to complete the soon-to-be registered name. As time passed, Foxy would more than live up to his name, as he would express himself in crafty ways.

I turned and walked from the dimly lit stable into the bright sunlight with the full realization that my life had changed dramatically. Owning and raising a stallion would be a unique experience. Although I had been exposed to an old Standardbred stallion named Claude Hanover, it was now totally up to me to shape and train this young colt. The end result would be my making, good or bad.

I heeded all of the advice I received from the experts, including the haunting, wise voice of old Mr Pigeau resting in the heavens. It urged my conscience to be careful. Whether I lucked out or had simply taken on the role of dominant herd leader from the beginning, Foxy never posed a risk throughout his entire life.

It was during this time that I met my husband. He was a shy man who felt uncomfortable in large crowds. Although he was never exposed to horses, marrying me meant marrying my lifestyle. He often teases me by telling people he lent me most of the money to purchase my first Morgan and look where it got him. Few good men would have given so unselfishly to encourage and participate in my passionate dream that only grew with time.

Foxy was to be my first training project of consequence, and I was very pleased with our progress. With just a few weeks to prepare, Foxy entered the weanling class at our regional breed show and took second place. He stood in a proud park position for the camera, seemingly dwarfed by the ribbon. As a yearling, he pushed the envelope further. With maturity came more awards, and at age two, he was pinned Junior Champion High Point Stallion. By his fourth year, Foxy had been trained to harness and was shown with an honourable degree of success. He was working under saddle at the time and came home with a ribbon hanging from the brow band. Success was sweet, especially being a homegrown training project. The critics who speculated my failure with this young stallion were to be proven wrong. In all, Foxy would earn more than 1,000 ribbons in the show arena during his career.

At age seven, while just entering his prime for competition, he fell ill with a lung condition. Foxy struggled to breathe. The diagnosis revealed that he had contracted a virus from a new horse that entered the stable. The veterinarian had been summoned on several occasions, treating the cough and congestion with a mixture of powders and syrups. As Foxy's condition deteriorated, I prayed for a recovery. It was then that I sought a second opinion in the hopes of salvaging my handsome young stallion.

Sympathizing with my plight, fellow owners recommended a young veterinarian that was gaining a reputation as being a good horse doctor. My current veterinarian would soon be retiring, so I decided to enlist the services of this new veterinarian. I was desperate to have any help at that point.

Dr Morrison drove into the stable yard and unloaded his black folding case of medical apparatus, along with an assortment of medicines from the back of his vehicle. After a brief introduction, I led him to Foxy's stall and awaited his diagnosis.

The news wasn't good. Foxy was struggling with a case of double pneumonia that seriously affected his ability to receive oxygen and exchange the carbon dioxide in his lungs. In order to determine how much damage the viral infection had already caused, Foxy was referred to the University of Guelph, Large Animals Admission.

A few days later, Foxy underwent a thorough examination at Guelph. The ravages of double pneumonia had left him with a permanent condition of chronic bronchitis. Never again would his wind be sound. With careful environmental management, there was a chance that he could return to some activity. Foxy was loaded in the trailer for the trip home.

We were advised that ideally he should never have seen the inside of a stable again, but of course that was not practical. Instead, we fashioned a small paddock to attach to the corner of his outer wall double Dutch door. It was to remain open year round so he could have the benefit of continual access to fresh air.

During that first winter following his return from Guelph, Foxy was put on a recipe of specially formulated medications to clear the airways. Coupled with the drugs was a regiment of light but regular exercise. Every morning before leaving for my desk job in the city, I would drive out to the farm. Since the best path to take Foxy on meant riding the shoulder of a busy service road, I strapped bicycle flashlights onto my stirrup irons, and I pulled a reflective safety vest over my riding jacket.

Off we would go into the darkness of early morning, heading west and then south toward the lake. At times, the wind would rudely slap my face and sting my hands that gripped the reins. On we would go at a steady, slow pace as our warm breath formed puffy clouds that rose in the clear, arcticlike air. By spring, his breathing had improved considerably. Despite the occasional cough, Foxy returned to his usual activities. It wasn't until years later when we met the respiratory veterinarian specialist again who had originally diagnosed Foxy's condition at Guelph did we learn that they had not expected Foxy to live another two years. Needless to say, they were thrilled to learn that he competed until age sixteen in the demanding show arena and remained healthy except for the occasional cough.

As Foxy adjusted to life in the open and began indulging himself in challenges, his new surroundings sharpened his mind as he planned an escape route. He was quick and mischievous of mind just like his name implied. They say that horses aren't logical in their thought processes, but I don't know if that was entirely true when it came to Foxy.

Foxy came up with an ingenious plan one day that would allow him to escape from his paddock as he eyed the lush pasture. At first, he practised with deliberate caution, standing on each strand of wire and trying to pull the fence down enough so he could walk over it. The new wire proved to be too tough for him, so he abandoned that plan. Finally, he chose the perfect escape to freedom. On a few occasions, this Houdini of the horse world was found grazing in blissful peace yards away from his private enclosure. When viewed from a distance, all doors were closed, and the fence appeared to be intact. We thought that Foxy had taken on a new sport of jumping. But we soon dismissed that idea since he was too smart for jumping. It would be too much effort.

As we opened his stall door from the stable and ventured out to his paddock, our eyes intently surveyed the fence line. Something looked suspicious at one corner of the enclosure beside the barn stone wall. As we drew closer, we discovered a large hole big enough for a horse to crawl under if it knew how. That is what was occupying Foxy's spare time. He was digging his escape route. You would have thought that he was a POW (Prisoner of War) like in the classic movie *The Great Escape*.

Since he had mastered that system of escape, we had to come up with a better plan to contain him. We decided to hot-wire his fence, both top and bottom, with electric fencing. Foxy still had one up on us with this new security addition. He knew when the shock box was plugged in and when it wasn't by listening for the monotonous *tick, tick* as the electric jolt pulsated through the wire. If he heard no *tick, tick*, he would wander over to his freshly covered hole and resume digging all over again.

After his great escape from the paddock, he was well versed in crawling under things. He wasn't the sort of horse you left unattended even with a stall guard in place. The contortionist that he was, Foxy would literally drop to his knees and crawl under the guard. He had been caught red-handed (hooves in this case) several times in this brazen attempt.

There wasn't really anything that Foxy wouldn't try if it took his fancy. Even stairs weren't an issue with him as our St Bernard dog named Tammy tugged on his lead shank and galloped up the hayloft stairs. Foxy would follow behind a hoof at a time. Realizing that he was now pursing her, Tammy dropped the shank. Foxy retreated back down to level ground as the pull on the shank released.

Foxy's tolerance to pain was high. On one warfare engagement, he battled another stallion whose door had been carelessly left unlocked. The stall housed a huge thoroughbred stallion that took it upon himself to rid the stable of this little pesky Morgan stud. The thoroughbred proceeded to tear down Foxy's door in a rage of contempt. We soon received an urgent call to come to the stable. When we arrived upon the scene, it looked like something straight out of a war zone. There was debris and blood splattered everywhere. Foxy stood exhausted and bleeding, but he had won the battle. Down the aisle, a veterinarian attended to the wounds of the sixteen-hand thoroughbred stallion, now trembling in the confusion and aftermath of battle. The horse was so traumatized that he was treated for shock, as well.

A few days later, I saddled Foxy up for some light exercise, rationalizing that it would be good for him to stretch some of his stiffened muscles. We started out at a leisurely walk with a small stumble here and there breaking the rhythm of the gait. There was little evidence to support any claim for suspicious lameness. The pasture field was rough, so the slight stumbles were ignored as nothing more than uneven terrain. We progressed to a trot and canter. Still, the stumbles continued. To be prudent, I reined him up and dismounted for further investigation. My eyes fixated on his left front leg. I was horrified to see blood gushing from a faint crack in his hoof wall. In his battle fatigue, it was suggested that his hoof had made contact with the stone of the stable wall, hence cracking his hoof on impact. Despite the obvious pain he must have endured while I was in the saddle, he never resisted any of my requests or displayed complaints with stalling or ears pinning. It would be a year of specialized farrier work, adding a bar shoe to stabilize the hoof. In the end, the hoof grew out normally, and no further intervention was necessary.

After Foxy totally recovered, plans were made to send him to a trainer for fine-tuning in harness. At the end of the advanced training period, Foxy came home with a much-desired extended trot. Unfortunately, it wasn't Foxy. The once mild-mannered and friendly stallion had turned into a crazed animal, literally climbing the walls of his stall. He fretted constantly, and we feared it was the equivalent of a mental breakdown. He had lost considerable weight and had no appetite. What had we done? A friend of mine who had worked at the racetrack suggested we get him a goat. We were desperate to try anything. We found a breeder and purchased a young goat. Within a week, Foxy started to respond. I dare say that Tinker the goat was Foxy's ultimate salvation.

Foxy and Tinker lived together all that summer. Foxy delighted in carrying poor Tinker around his stall by the scruff of his neck as he lifted him out of his hay manger. The wailing Tinker would call to us for rescue.

Later that year, we decided to try another trainer to put more finishing touches on Foxy's Western discipline skills. Although somewhat nervous over our decision, this time, Foxy had his companion at his side, so off he went to school. Another incident of stall latch failure released a dominant alpha-personality gelding from his stall. He headed straight for Foxy's stall, as he was determined to have more than words with the new stud in the barn. A horrendous fight ensued. Foxy's sharp toe clip had twisted sideways and punctured the sole of his hoof. This meant a layup again. At least this time, the injury wasn't as severe.

Being a master of escape much like his buddy Foxy, Tinker managed to find his way out of the stall. He discovered the grain room, where he gorged himself literally to death. Poor Tinker was found in a heap outside of Foxy's stall. On our visit that day, we came upon the tragic scene. It was a pitiful sight. Foxy stood by his door, pawing endlessly and trying to pull Tinker back into the stall. There was a gap of about six inches at the bottom of the stall door. Without a companion, Foxy went off his feed for a few days. Refusing to eat, he stood with his head pressed into the corner of his stall. Tinker was buried at that farm, and Foxy came home.

There was never a dull moment with Foxy around. The wheels were always turning.

We had arrived for a parade one Saturday in early December. While I was dashing about in the change room of the trailer, zipping up the leggings of my chaps, Bob was outside finishing up saddling Foxy. Somehow, Foxy slipped the confines of his halter while tethered to the side of the trailer. He decided to go for a stroll through the crowded parking lot of the schoolyard we were parked in. Foxy's leisurely stroll soon advanced to an all-out road trot. As I fastened the buckle of my chaps in place, I could hear Bob's frantic calls trailing off in the distance. As I swung the door of the tack room open, there was poor Bob holding onto the cinch strap and pacing alongside Foxy. In true horsemanship response, ignoring the plight of the exhausted sideways partner, I yelled back, "Don't let go!" If you have ever tried to keep up with a road-trotting horse, you can imagine the next scene. I had never seen Bob's feet fly by so fast. One would have thought he was trying out for a world-record sprint as he bounced along beside the horse, his knees clearly engaged. Foxy moved up his gait a notch. Bob took hold of the saddle horn for more stability. His feet touched the ground briefly with every bounce of the horse's stride as he flew along side the horse. I'm certain that Foxy was having one hearty horselaugh. A small group of us banded together to form a human corral of sorts. It worked, and we finally put an end to the wayward stallion's joke. Bob's rib cage heaved so hard that I thought his heart might stop right there. We completed the tacking up and rode the parade route without incident.

For anyone who competes in the show ring, there are always moments that stick hard and fast in our thoughts. As they can never be repeated, these treasures of time past are locked safely away. One of the most vivid exploits of this horse for us was during his show career and his entry in the Justin Morgan Performance classes. This class is a stamina-driven event.

Foxy was always rated as the underdog in these events, especially with his handicap of debilitated, sensitive airways. For most horses, this restriction of lung capacity would hamper, if not nullify, a horse's effort in the show ring, never mind a race. The year that Foxy finished second in 90 degree weather remains as fresh in my mind today as it was at the moment.

Foxy had competed in fourteen classes. Some were line classes prior to the scheduled final event of the show, which was the Justin Morgan Performance class. We cooled him as best we could from the day's demands. We poured buckets of slightly warm water over him and used sweat scrappers to draw the remaining beads of water and salt from his coat. He was pronounced ready for the big event.

The first segment of this final class was the half-mile race under saddle. That year, I had convinced one of the top youth riders to mount up for this race on Foxy. As the horses jockeyed into position, the race was called with the drop of a small hand flag. Off they went as their riders hollered to them to lower their haunches and push off. Foxy responded immediately. Everyone bunched together, trying to find space on the preferable rail position. At the second turn of the track were the stables off to the right. I had forewarned the rider that Foxy might drift to the outside when they approached that turn. Sure enough, Foxy started to drift wide. Instead of checking him back and driving him farther in, the jockey decided to push around the other horses. He had a lot more ground to make up by following this tactic. When asked, Foxy started to flatten his frame and pull away from the herd of horses. We watched from the base of the caller's tower as Foxy began to mow down his rivals. The game little horse named Danell's Nova Don had taken a respective lead early on and was banking on keeping it. Under a determined drive from above, Foxy continued to dig deep within and reach further as his nostrils flared to maximum effort. It soon became a two-horse race, and everyone screamed wildly as the horses thundered down to the wire. Foxy was in hot pursuit, but he was running out of track and ticks on the stopwatch to catch Don before the wire. Foxy had churned up the dirt in a deliberate attempt to outrun the others, who were now fading in their strides with exhaustion. As his hooves cupped the deep earth beneath him, Foxy drove ahead. Only the tail of one horse lay between him and victory. As the distance began to disappear rapidly and as the two horses struggled down the track, the roar of the crowd became deafening. My voice was strained as I called to Foxy to keep trying. I prayed that he could hear my pleas above the sea of screams. "Come on, Foxy," I cried to him repeatedly. Within a couple of yards before they passed under the wire, Foxy reached the throatlatch of Nova's Don. Time had run out, and Foxy had to be content as the runner-up. Don had held on to take the winner's circle.

Foxy's sides heaved in fatigue as his rider dismounted, and the saddle was changed. We walked slowly over to the show ring, where I mounted up and entered the second division of this event, the pleasure class. We dropped down a gear and went to business, finishing first this time. Foxy's manners were impeccable as he relaxed to my feel of the rein and sleepy roll of my seat in the saddle.

As we trotted out of the ring, his work collar was laid on the ground with the rest of his heavy leather harness. Stripped of his saddle and bridle, the work collar was turned upside down and slipped over his broad head. We rotated the heavily padded collar into place at the base of his neck, the shining steel hames reaching upward to the honey blue sky of late afternoon. As we finished harnessing, we waited to be called up for hooking to the stone boat for the final leg of the event.

Our number was called, and I picked up the lines and encouraged Foxy to walk forward. The stone boat lay in the middle of the track as I walked Foxy by the concrete-laden sled and positioned him for hooking.

He started to anticipate the pull as he agitated slightly, lifting his hind feet, one hoof at a time, in preparation. The traces were attached to the strapping whiffletree that jingled with the movement of the horse. The final drop of the pin to attach the whiffletree to the stone boat was made, and Foxy was given the command. "Pull!"

Foxy leaned into the brute collar as he dug the toes of his hooves into the track. He hopped a couple of steps, freeing the sled from its stationary post before driving his hips in a steady, even pull. His head bowed low as he gained momentum. In fact, he became so confident that he began trotting with the stone boat sledding behind. I leaned on the lines while asking him to halt. He was so strong by this point that the heels of my boots ploughed their own telltale track in the dirt as I braced to contain his enthusiasm. He halted, and the pin was released. Foxy had pulled more than the required distance.

The overall results were close, but they were not enough for Foxy to be totally victorious. The nod went to the courageous little gelding, Nova Don. Still, I was more than proud of Foxy's endurance and heart. Many people who witnessed these two horses duelling head-to-head would remember this competition for a long time. I can still hear the people screaming and hanging on the rail with excitement so long ago.

"The Fox," as he was sometimes called, was a horse of character and comedic proportions with high cranial intelligence for an equine. There were so many daily occasions where he would make me crack a smile. One particular moment was at a horse show at a fall fair when a rather inebriated fellow approached me and began to harass me. I was mounted on Foxy at the time, and we were making our way to the warm-up ring for the upcoming Western pleasure class. Bob had gone ahead to check the ring situation, so it was just Foxy and me in this rather deserted area of the fairgrounds. The members of the security staff were nowhere to be found, so I was left to deal with the situation as best I could.

As I pressed with a light leg aid, Foxy quietly lifted his front hoof and placed it hard and square on the man's foot. The guy must have been in excruciating pain, only it was dulled by the amount of liquor he had consumed. Foxy never moved and continued to press down as I leaned my hip in that direction. I finally relented to the man's pleas and moved Foxy forward and away. I didn't steal a glance over my shoulder but instead deliberately ignored him as he howled in obvious suffering. A smirk of sweet revenge crept onto my lips and into my mind as we jogged down the track. Foxy and I went on to win the Western pleasure class.

Outside the show arena, Foxy and I enjoyed nature's pathways. It was a nice escape from the boredom of ring work.

As we followed a narrow path of foliage that lazily edged along the creek bed, we decided to venture in the slow-running water. The cool splash of water on his belly was a welcomed relief on that hot summer day. I guided Foxy through the stream of water. Suddenly, Foxy disappeared beneath me as the sandy floor dropped away, and we sank in response. My first reaction was that of shock at being dunked, and I was frightened. But I soon realized that, yes, Foxy could swim. I was still saddle bound when Foxy's hooves touched the bottom of the creek for the second time as he pushed and lifted the bulk of his body. Securing his footing and firmly claiming the creek bottom, we headed up the grassy bank, slipping and sliding as we went. Totally soaked from our immersion, we had been initiated into the rite of bona fide trail buddies.

A month before his twenty-fifth birthday, Foxy was diagnosed with an incurable condition. Saying goodbye would be intolerable but inevitable as the months passed.

I had become increasingly suspicious when Foxy seemed to ignore the mares that passed by his private paddock as he was led to the adjacent pasture. That characteristic raised head and arched neck remained low and stiff. My first thought was that he had suffered some sort of injury to his neck and that it would eventually ease with the help of medication. There was no improvement. I became increasingly worried when I noticed a stagger in his once proud gait. He was having trouble with his balance. I thought perhaps he had a small inner ear problem as I searched for a possible diagnosis. I made an appointment, and a series of tests were performed to manipulate the limbs. At the end of the examination, the prognosis was grim. Harry advised me that it was not good, and that I should consider euthanasia, the sooner the better. My breathing became weak and shallow as I struggled to listen to Harry's words. Foxy looked at me with a curious tilt of his head as tears welled up in my eyes. It was spring, and the weather was lovely. I just couldn't let him go without one more summer. I promised that he wouldn't have to endure another winter, but I felt that I owed him the summer.

Every day was special from then on. His birthday was marked with much fanfare. He had his fill of apples and carrots and stood contently as he was petted and praised by the many that came to visit.

The stagger of his gait was pronounced, but it didn't depress old Foxy's mood. Feeling defeated or sorry for himself was not in Foxy's nature. Instead, he mapped out every inch of his paddock, learning where to step. He was careful and deliberate when he walked. He was turned out on level pasture ground to help with his impaired balance. He didn't seem in pain and spent the warm summer days grazing and calling to his mares in the far meadow.

With the coolness of fall, I had to face the reality of his disease and the hazards it posed. Harry didn't want me to carry any guilt if I allowed Foxy to stay the winter. There was a high probability of an ice-related injury. I would not entertain scenarios of him falling and becoming unable to stand, possibly suffering hypothermia or the fracture of a leg. I knew that it was the most humane thing to do, but still it tugged so hard at my heart. Even now, that day brings sadness when I reflect on my decision.

Personally, I couldn't bear being a witness to his final moments. I made a tearful goodbye and left the deed to my veterinarian. As the tranquilizer was slowly injected, I gave Foxy one last pat on the neck and walked away.

Someone placed a single red rose on the freshly covered grave that afternoon. He was at peace now.

Chapter 12

My Horses, My Heaven on Earth

Ginger

How excited I was the day I led Hobbition Tinuviel, better known as Ginger, home to our barn! It was the beginning of our successful breeding program. That brisk walk she had is etched forever in my comfort shed of memories. She kept me at a jog just to match her stride as she was led away down the road. I had an extra spring to my step as I proudly walked Ginger into the stable yard after our short stroll. Although thin from nursing her recently weaned foal, she was pretty. Her carrot-red mane contrasted handsomely with her deep burgundy coat. Her large, soft eyes reflected her inner beauty and kindness of heart. I had great expectations for Ginger as I led her into a freshly bedded stall. She dropped her nose and nuzzled into the sweet straw, signifying her acceptance of her new home. Ownership was now permanent, and she would be with us the rest of her days.

Ginger had been on lease to the same Morgan farm from which I had purchased Foxy. They were now located just around the corner from the old stable we were leasing at the time. Ginger was scheduled to return to New York when the opportunity arose for me to purchase my first foundation mare. I had researched her background and knew that the bloodlines of Vigilmarch and the famous Merrylegs would give me the athletic Morgans I so admired. The deal was transacted, and the papers were transferred.

Ginger was foaled on March 27, 1987, at Mabel Owens's farm in Massachusetts. She was owned by Rosemary and David Papayanopulos of Huntington, New York. She was the first to carry the Hobbiton prefix, fashioned after characters in the popular trilogy fantasy stories from *Lord of the Rings*, i.e., the Hobbits. Ginger was by the first son of Vigilmarch, Bro-Rock March On and out of the great mare, Merry Bellsinda, a pedigree that reaches back through Merry Knox and Belldale to the likes of Meade and the famous old government mare, Florette. Although these family names are unfamiliar to the general public, they are well recognized among Morgan horse fanciers. These lines of horses were renowned for their stamina, completing gruelling 300-mile endurance cavalry tests, and they were bred to get the job done.

After settling into life with us that first year and gaining back show weight, Ginger was loaded in the trailer, and she made her debut in the show ring the following summer. She was accompanied by the seasoned campaigner, Foxy. He seemed to enjoy the company on the road. A highlight from Ginger's brief show career involved a Western pleasure class at one of the fall fairs. A light breeze with just a twist of coolness brushed against my face as Ginger and I jogged into the ring that afternoon. Ginger met life in the ring with unfazed indifference. She was happy and content doing her thing. She could be trotting along a busy show rail amid the roar of whirling rides and cotton candy or just snoozing along a sleepy, peaceful trail at sunset. Ginger loped on command as the ring steward bellowed out the judge's required gait to the riders in the ring. She backed readily for the judge and stood patiently in the lineup when the class was called. She had performed with impeccable manners and ease. Still, it was the great Aristippi that was favoured to win. Tippi, as she was affectionately known, was a world champion and knew the show ring better than anyone. All eyes rested on Tippi. We stood in quiet anticipation, waiting to hear the placings echo from the loudspeakers poised high above us on the tall wooden poles. "In first place, congratulations to number twenty-one, Hobbiton Tinuviel, owned by the Trillium Morgan Horse Farm and ridden today in victory by Catherine Sampson!" the announcer rang out from the booth. At first, I didn't move. I couldn't fathom that my novice Western pleasure horse had taken top honours. I shook myself into reality as I pressed lightly on Ginger's wide foaling barrel and urged her forward. We jogged up to the ribbon bearer, who reached over and pinned the first-place ribbon onto Ginger's bridle. The judge approached us and congratulated us on our win. She told us that Ginger was the only horse that worked off of a relaxed rein. The ribbon danced in the breeze of our lope of victory as we passed through the gate, exiting the ring.

Ginger retired to the role of motherhood shortly after that season. In all, Ginger produced ten offspring consisting of eight colts and two fillies, her last foal arriving in 1992. As time went by in the foaling box, my original blueprint to produce an athletic Morgan was borne out with Ginger's first foal for us, Trillium Reflection, by Lauralee

Foxy Man. Reflection more than lived up to our dream for a good trotting Morgan. He eventually won the Canadian Morgan Horse Club National Reserve Championship based primarily on his racing endeavours in Vermont. He excels in road hack classes, too, and like his mom, he has a powerful, ground-covering walk that makes life lonely out on the trail in the company of others.

Besides being an adoring mother, Ginger's biggest attraction was her personality. Everyone loved her. Over the years, she had gathered her own exclusive fan club of admirers, mostly young, impressionable children or timid individuals. With her delightful, warm, inviting nature, these people quickly overcame their fear of the horse's titanic proportions. Needless to say, her favourite "people" activity was parades. It was difficult to keep her in a straight line on the parade route as she walked stirrup-to-stirrup with her stablemate Foxy. She often wandered over to the waiting crowds with her ears pricked forward, hoping to be petted. And there was one special little trick she had that delighted both the young and old.

Breeder Mabel Owens once said that Ginger almost went through life with the nickname "Tongue." She had a fetish for sticking her tongue out of the left side of her mouth whenever someone approached her. You couldn't possibly ignore it. In fact, she wanted very much for you to stroke her tongue. She would cock her head in the desired position, encouraging you to pet it while smiling at the same time. Her lips pulled back, creating a silly grin. It was somewhat embarrassing when she was judged on line in the total atmosphere of serious competition. She wanted to get the judge's attention, so as if on cue, out popped that pink tongue when he or she approached. We gave up scolding her for it and eventually just accepted this peculiarity as part of her endearing character. She had this habit right from birth according to Mabel, and it stuck with her all her days.

Like her son Reflection, Ginger, too, made an exceptional trail horse that could outwalk any horse on the farm. She wasn't content to hold back because slow walking wasn't her thing. When you walked, *you walked!*

In the spring of 1992, Ginger presented us with her last foal sired by Trillium Samson. From day one, this bright fellow followed everyone around without the benefit of traditional training to lead. Just being with people seems natural. He, Trillium Brass Buttons, definitely inherited his mom's charm and personality.

It is clear that Ginger's disposition and manner was infectious and inheritable, as so many of her offspring display it. It is funny how a Morgan cross named Ginger entered my early life, and later on I would own a purebred Morgan whose pet name was also Ginger. These subtle coincidences would continue to unfold as time went on.

This story wouldn't be complete without the inclusion of two other very special horses. Since their remaining years were so intertwined, it is only appropriate to tell their stories together.

It was May 23, 1969, when H-Loli entered the world. It was not in the confines of a deep-bedded straw foaling stall with today's technology and fancy monitors or foal watchers looking on to ensure a safe delivery. Rather, she came in a more humble way, born on the open and rugged plains of Wyoming. Without benefit of shelter or human intervention, she braved the elements and constant danger from predators.

Intrigue and Loli

She was a daughter of the famous Chingadero, the stallion with his pale cremello coloring that was considered to be white at the time. Chingadero in part was credited for a catalyst of change in the registry rules for the breed of the day. Years later, the infamous "white rule" would be rescinded after decades of controversy. The white rule, in effect, banned registry of Morgans carrying white markings above the knee or hock, except for facial markings. A Morgan considered to be "high white" was left in limbo as to the recording of its parentage. These orphan Morgans were considered grade horses, as they did not meet the breed standard for registry at that time.

H-Loli was foaled on the property of the Cross Ranch and bred by George A. Cross and Sons. She carried two distinctive brands; there was one on her neck and another on her hip. She was line bred to Flyhawk with four crosses to Warhawk on her pedigree. Much like her other siblings by Chingadero, she was solid black in colour with no markings. Though not a big horse by the stick, she was tough and resilient like many others from that breeding program. And she produced bigger than herself.

This family line of Morgan horses were all considered to be tough fighters of mishap and injury. H-Loki would attest to this survival instinct later on in her life. She would have four other owners as she travelled from the mountainous rocky ranges of Wyoming to the flat lands of Iowa and then on to New York before entering Canada in 1979.

In the late summer of 1980, I had an opportunity to visit Jack Reeves' Chestnut Hill Morgan Farm and view the horses listed on their dispersal sale catalogue. It wasn't long before I focused my attention on the lone little black mare with a large buckskin colt at her side. As I approached the somewhat timid mare, it was her large, clear eyes that attracted me most to her. Those eyes and the intelligence and good nature they reflected convinced me that she was indeed special from all the rest in the pasture of quality Morgans.

Her sturdy build and inch-by-inch Morgan qualities came through in her outward appearance and mild manner. She traveled with good motion. This was a trait she had inherited from her dam according to the late Albert Cross. Loli's hooves never saw steel and remained durable and unmarred until very late in her life. Her disposition was that of her sire, old Chingadero. In his letter to me, Abe Cross remarked that Chingadero was the best-natured Morgan they had ever bred out of hundreds of foals they produced over the years at their ranch.

Loli had been bred back to Clear River Phantom, a son of Merry Knox, that spring of 1980, and she was due to be weaned from the foal she had at that time. Soon, the purchase was made, and I welcomed Loli to our farm that fall. It would be a remarkable journey in her life coming to Trillium. It was to be her final home. She produced multiple offspring of kind, willing temperaments and unquestionable Morgan type, grit, and talent.

I always believed in giving the broodmares a rest once in a while to rejuvenate them regardless of the gamble for rebreeding the next season. It perhaps is not a sound financial decision, but it is rather a more humane one. Following this program, Loli was not bred every year during her most fertile years as a broodmare. However, she did produce eleven registered offspring in her lifetime, most notably leaving behind her greatest legacy in the farm's leading sire, Trillium Samson. Her very last offspring, at age twenty-five, was a black filly named Trillium Lady of Intrigue. She was sired by none other than Serenity Intrigue. The list of grand offspring of H-Loli is long and impressive, with many of them achieving grand champion and national status, such as Trillium's Chantilly Lace, Trillium Arioso, and Trillium Classic.

Colour did come through from time to time with Loli. She produced three gold mint palominos and a couple of honey buckskin Morgans. Mostly, she produced bay or chestnut in colour. It didn't seem to matter what colour she produced, as all of her foals were excellent both in Morgan type, smarts, and ability.

Never a saddle or harness horse, Loli was still one of the most popular Morgans at the farm even though she was just a companion and broodmare. But what a broodmare!

It was her demeanour that won people over on first encounter and of course that eye, full of life and clarity. She drew a crowd like a magnet at the farm's many public events. She was special beyond her size. She was ebony in colour and occasionally with an adorable foal at her side. She was a most trusting horse who would let the veterinarian stitch a flap of skin on her face without the benefit of freezing or restraint, as she was so heavy in foal. And in the last year of her life and as testimony to her courage, she endured the devastation of massive infection, paralysis, and the enormous healing process left in its wake.

Seventeen days before reaching her thirty-first birthday, Loli faced a crisis that threatened her very existence. The twenty-eight-year matriarch and grand dam of our farm was stricken with a near-fatal bout of cellulitis, or in layperson's terms, a massive infection.

On the evening of May 6, 2000, while Bob and I were attending a family celebration, our assistant stable manager at the time was volunteering to do the evening barn check. During her rounds, she noticed that Loli had not shown much attention to her feed that night. She decided to investigate further and noticed that the old mare was drooling excessively. Following our medical routine in the stable, her first priority was to take the mare's temperature. Loli spiked at 103 degrees Fahrenheit, which was reason for concern. Dr Harry Morrison was informed immediately of the problem.

We cut short our dinner engagement and arrived at the farm shortly before Harry turned down the stable lane.

He probed the mare's neck and throatlatch, looking for any clues about her affliction. After a thorough examination of the mare and with careful inspection of her mouth, nothing seemed to present itself as the source of a possible infection.

At first suspicious of a tooth abscess, he ruled it out after noting the excellent condition of the mare's teeth. This was remarkable, especially considering her advanced age. Maybe it was a tumour? One last palpation of the exterior mandible and cheek area only revealed a very slight swelling of the left cheek. As a preventative measure, he administered a series of injections to the mare to help reduce the fever and combat the infection.

By the following morning, Loli had deteriorated dramatically. The left side of her face had tripled in size, with severe swelling making haltering impossible. Eating or drinking was hampered to the point where she could no longer obtain any nourishment or fluid. Dr Morrison was summoned again.

Some of the medications from the previous night had adequately controlled the fever, but her heart rate and respiration were still elevated. Dehydration was now a real concern, as well.

Ice packs were applied to the cheek area, but this seemed to supply little or no relief. A new set of medications was administered. This time, the barrage of drugs used included antihistamines, more penicillin, Banamine®, Tribrissen®, Hemo-15®, electrolytes, and phenylbutazone.

By the third day, Loli's eye showed signs of distress, and a weepy discharge was very evident. The swelling was advancing and closing her left eye, travelling as far as the base of her ear down to her muzzle. It had involved the entire left side of her face and appeared to have completed its journey of infection. The veterinarian had termed this as walling off.

Although her vitals had stabilized, she was unable to eat or drink anything. Blood was drawn and rushed to the laboratory for analysis. In consultation with the veterinarian, I decided that if the mare did not show any improvement within twenty-four hours, there would be no alternative but to end her misery humanely. At that point, I set in motion arrangements to have a gravesite prepared.

It was a grey morning on May 9 as the backhoe completed its job, and I prepared to make my farewell to Loli with a lot of tears. Dr Morrison was to arrive shortly and was ready to give Loli the needle of "big sleep." Nothing much had changed as I wept at the sight of the oozing serum seeping through Loli's stretched and tired flesh. Her pathetic face was now unrecognizable as one belonging to a horse. Her nose and lower lip were paralysed with the pressure that had built up so aggressively that it left her with a crooked muzzle. Her left eye was now tightly closed and weeping with mucus.

The laboratory results were in, and to everyone's amazement, everything was rated as normal, including her white cell count. Her hemoglobin was at 162, and her WBC count at an unremarkable 5.5. The mystery of her illness deepened.

A gloomy-faced veterinarian and his assistant arrived at the farm midmorning. Harry wanted to see his patient for a final assessment before giving her the injection of death. As he hopped over the paddock fence, Loli became suspicious and trotted wildly around the enclosure before retreating to her open stall. Harry followed only to find the old horse attempting to chew some hay from her wall rack.

This was the very first time she had been observed trying to eat anything since her illness first appeared on May 6.

For an hour, Harry patiently waited as his attention was drawn to Loli's eating process. He watched for good excursion of the mandibles and noted the fact that she wasn't expelling any hay. She had managed to chew well, showing no signs of an abscessed tooth. She swallowed the hay with difficulty.

A small amount of grain was offered to the now starving mare. To everyone's delight, she devoured that, as well. A garden hose was inserted into the corner of her mouth, allowing enough water to make its way to the back of her throat. She eagerly gulped the water down.

In the final assessment, Harry just couldn't give up on Loli. As he put it, "If she's not ready to go, then I don't think we should quit, either." And so a new course of action to battle her affliction began.

He injected her with a massive amount of steroids, and more penicillin was in order. My concern with the steroid treatment was in how it may affect an old chronic laminitis problem the mare had developed over the previous couple of years. It was a gamble, but it was worth trying since we had few other options.

Hot compresses from an Epsom Salt solution were to be applied daily as often as possible to try to draw out the poison forming in the giant and growing abscess.

By May 11, Harry decided to see if the abscess was ripe enough to lance. He inserted a needle into the most prominent site, which brought forth immediate results. He made a small incision with a scalpel at first, and the site began to drain in earnest. He dispatched the scalpel a second time and a made a slightly wider incision. This would be the beginning of ridding the site of infection as the thick pus flowed unrestricted down her cheek.

The incision site was flushed routinely with hydrogen peroxide and Betadine®. Next, large abdominal sterile pads dressed with nitrofurazone ointment were applied and held in place with 3M™ Vetwrap Bandaging Tape and hospital surgical tape.

Although her face was disfigured and paralysis of her lower left muzzle was still evident, the tenacity this old girl displayed was remarkable. If it was to be her last hurrah, she was going out as a fighter.

The next day, Loli appeared to have slipped somewhat as her appetite waned, and drinking on her own without the aid of the hose had tapered off. A sinking feeling came over everyone who had worked so hard to care for Loli these past few days. The hole still stood silent like the Grim Reaper, and I sought Dr Morrison's advice once again.

Dutifully, Harry arrived later that morning and reassessed Loli. He made another incision to the lower mandible area, and more of the same thick, putrid infection began to stream out. It was as though a tap had been suddenly turned on. The stench from the festering mass permeated the air of the stable, and more of the dead tissue would have to be cut away each day. Still, the intensive care giving had to continue if Loli was to survive.

Harry had prepared everyone for the horrors of what lay ahead. As predicted, Loli's hide and flesh began to die and slough off, leaving her face resembling raw hamburger. The most disgusting task was left to me to tackle. Controlling my impulse to vomit at the sight of rotting flesh and horrific stench, I started the process of removing the dead hide from her face. I was fearful of cutting into live tissue. As the hide continued to die off, I continued to cut away at the skin, exposing the underlying muscle, tendon, and wasting matter. By May 16, she had lost the whole left side of her face with just a few patches of hide connecting the large cheek to the muzzle. The ravages of the infection had left just blood vessels and muscle behind.

Miraculously, by May 19, all traces of the infection had gone, and the paralysis to her nose and lower lip had disappeared. A thick, granular base of fresh skin was forming rapidly. The best news of all was that the grave could finally be filled in minus the horse.

On May 23, Loli reached a milestone that no one thought would ever happen. She celebrated her thirty-first birthday with lots of carrots, apples, and love.

Loli had lost a considerable amount of weight during her ordeal. The 14.3-hand mare dropped to 860 pounds. Still, she was incredibly bright and now more than ever was determined to regain her lost condition and weight with an appetite resembling that of a hungry wolf.

The healing process was a daily wonder. By June 11, Loli had recovered most of her flesh, including new hide. No one could have imagined that she would produce so much new skin, let alone hair, too.

Nature helped, as well. With a cooler than usual spring, flies were not abundant and spared us from having to deal with a maggot-infestation problem of the wound area, as well.

More than 100 hours of care had been lovingly spent on helping Loli come back from a fate she wasn't ready to accept. A medicine trunk had been donated to house the many bandaging materials and other medical supplies that were required for her treatment. Reading over the somewhat weighty and detailed daily entries in the stable logbook, resurrected old feelings of despair, hope, and joy. Each turn of the page brought back the terrible details this medical anomaly had presented. I could almost smell the decaying flesh as I read through the text. It is a distinctively sweet and disgusting smell of decomposition that stays with you. It is easily recognizable once you've been exposed to it.

During the early stages of her illness, I wouldn't allow photographs to be taken, even in the interest of medical evidence. I wanted to remember her whole and in good health as I struggled with the reality that she might not pull through. It was only as the healing took hold that a camera lens was employed to document the recovery process. I still marvel at the body's ability to reconstruct so perfectly in Loli's case.

Our stable journal recorded the inventory of medicines used to maintain Loli throughout her ordeal. Through the course of her treatment, ninety-eight rolls of 3M™ Vetwrap Bandaging Tape were used, as well as forty-eight rolls of surgical tape, 148 eight-by-ten inch sterile abdominal pads, thirty-five smaller sterile pads, twenty surgical scrub sponges, 5.25 litres of hydrogen peroxide, 5.5 litres of

Betadine®, 3.5 kilograms of nitrofurazone ointment, 3.5 grams of ophthalmic ointment, and other sundry items.

It had been quite a roller coaster ride all the way. Twice the mare was considered for euthanasia; twice she showed the grit and will to live that shamed us all to have even considered the possibility of ending her courageous life.

Although the nursing skills may have been rudimentary, Loli would not have healed so well and so rapidly without the many volunteers who offered to care for her. It was a round-the-clock caregiving routine. Loli would not have lived had it not been for the wisdom and advice of her attending veterinarian, either. Loli's companion, Intrigue, the Morgan stallion would continue to comfort her in her few remaining days that year.

...

Foaled on May 8, 1970, Serenity Intrigue was one of three full siblings. Besides being one of the last sons of the great Vigilmarch, his notable distinction from this culmination of bloodlines was that he was the only producing sire and full brother to Val's Terry. Adored by his fans, the flashy gelding with the flaxen mane and tail affectionately known simply as Terry was considered by many to be the greatest show horse in Morgan history. He won an incredible eighteen world championships.

Intrigue graced the show ring briefly, winning his share of ribbons and championships but only in the shadow of his famous brother. Mostly, his value was perceived to be in the breeding shed, where he stood at stud in South Carolina and Georgia before rocking to the movement of the moving box stall on his route north to Canada and home to Trillium in the spring of 1990. After all, he was the only one, other than his sister, Serenity Victoria, who was capable of passing on genes that may yet produce another Terry some day.

Intrigue sired fifty-nine registered offspring during his lifetime and most likely countless others. At age twenty-eight, he sired his last foal, the filly Trillium Intrigues Spirit, who crossed the Atlantic to pasture in the heather lands of Scotland.

I clearly remember the day when the grand stallion first arrived and walked off the van into the yard after his long journey from Atlanta. I had made the purchase sight unseen, basing my decision solely on his excellent bloodlines. It was a risk I took purchasing a stallion of age, but I have no regrets. He was everything I expected and more.

His stable name was chosen by one of the boarders the very first day he was in our stable. She kept referring to him as "Studley Do Right." It stuck, and most people just referred to him as Studley in the end.

Intrigue was a real gentleman and easy breeder. His mane, tail, and forelock were long and abundant. He was undeniably Morgan in every sense. His head with its chiselled and refined features reflected his intelligent mind and good breeding. His hooves were solid and unblemished. He possessed clean, dense bone and a strong hip that everyone described as "the butt walk" when in motion. That wide, moving, driving hind would be a trait he would pass on to a number of his offspring.

Intrigue would sire fabulous offspring for us over the years, such as Trillium Precious Memory, Trillium Symphony of Fire, Trillium Independence, and Trillium Peppermint Patty to name just a few. All of his get are talented and full of personality. They are very clever horses, bold and willing. They are also enduring horses, tough for the competition with stamina that just will not falter.

Many of his offspring entered the field of competitive ride. One son held the distinct honour of leading a fox hunt near our nation's capital. Yet others were successful in the hunter division. Another son is noted as a distinguished police horse in the southern United States, and more offspring are remembered as brilliant roadsters and pleasure horses.

Even in his twilight days, the glorious stallion still stood with that typical regal Vigilmarch air that no one could deny him. To the end, he kept his promise and guarded old Loli with his entire being. He shared his hay and beet pulp, shared his water bucket, and kept watch over her tired body, as weary as he was, too.

On the early morning of November 23, 2000, with temperatures plummeting to an unseasonable minus 10 degrees Celsius, I opened the stable door and turned off the alarm. I began the morning chores as I had done with regularity every morning. It was the American Thanksgiving holiday, and in a way, I, too, was giving thanks to these two American-bred Morgans for the last time. The routine was kept the same, but this was no ordinary day. It would be the last morning that I would feed and water two old and dearly loved friends, H-Loli and Serenity Intrigue.

We often joked about them as being "the old folks, Grandma and Grandpa," and the silly sign posted by their reserved paddock fence announcing, "An old stud and a cute filly live here." It gave us all a chuckle.

Soon, the stable would be quiet. There was only the sound of my soft whimpering and private tears as I waited for the veterinarian and backhoe to come and do their respective solemn duties.

I hugged Loli and cradled her with my arms wrapped around her neck for a long farewell. I had shared her life for twenty years, never with complaint but always with wonderment and gratitude. I can never recall a time of reprimand for an infraction. They say no one is perfect, but Loli had been an exception when it came to obedience, trust, and tolerance.

She had been one of our foundation mares and was without doubt the best. She had come through so much this past spring. She had battled a massive infection of her face that almost ended her life. Ironically, her heroic story of healing published in a national equine magazine would make the newsstands this very same day, November 23, 2000.

Intrigue, on the other hand, still stood defiant against being pampered. He only wanted to safeguard his sacred mare. I let him keep his stallion ways and snuck a gentle pat of his long, thick, flowing mane when he wasn't looking. How sad it seemed that the sassy fat stud who was like a Hoover at feed times would no longer shine in our stable after eleven years here at the farm.

It had been more than a year since we first had thoughts of ending his loneliness and misery when he seemingly lost all interest in eating and instead spent his days languishing and lying in his stall, making few attempts to rise. Harry, our veterinarian, made the suggestion of moving him to the open stall paddock that H-Loli occupied at the time. The theory was that having more room and access to an open paddock twenty-four hours a day would be beneficial for his aching joints. Reluctant to put the veteran stallion with the old broodmare, we decided it was worth a try, as euthanasia was our only other option. Within a week, the old boy had found a reason to live again. He had a job to do, and he never looked back.

It was Loli who had accepted the cranky old man and brought him much pleasure in companionship. They soon became inseparable. You couldn't take one away for grooming without the other tagging along. If momentarily out of sight, each would pace and whinny frantic calls of location to each other until they were reunited.

There is a very human message here that should not be ignored when we think of the elderly and the loneliness that besets many. These two old horses found a realm of safety and a feeling of being wanted again. It was the gift of companionship they needed to keep them happy and active and to be able to enjoy their lives for as long as they had left, be it ever so brief.

Stiff with the ravages of arthritis, the old stallion still shuffled along, standing over Loli like an old soldier protecting his mate. She would lay for hours in the wet sand paddock, finding relief for her old laminitis hooves.

His arthritis had advanced, making it almost impossible to trim his hooves. He was loaded up on painkillers the day prior to the farrier's appointment with the farm. On one particular date with the farrier, Intrigue went down in the aisle and couldn't rise. He lay there sprawled out on the rubber mat for two hours as other horses made a crooked path around his quiet, prostrate body. A defeated, soft nicker erupted from the old stallion when the horses walked by. It wasn't until a fourth person arrived that we were able to help him rise to his feet. After that, a makeshift sling was fashioned using the stall walls in the horse trailer to aid in his support.

Hooves were raised barely off the ground using a pulley of sorts as his tired body dropped into the webbing straps that held him in for balance. The farrier worked quickly to trim away the excess wall of his hooves as I patted his masculine neck and soothed his pain with my sympathetic whispering. We knew that soon this part of his maintenance would be unbearable for him.

How much more could we ask these valiant horses, now in their thirties, to endure without it being a crime of conscience to let them go on? So it had been mutually agreed that the two would go together, peacefully and painlessly.

Every day was like the last as I watched the two old horses comfort each other in their obvious continuing pain. The medications were losing their effectiveness. With that cold cruel wind blowing from the north and the ground cover freezing faster, the decision to spare these wonderful Morgans from the grips of winter became overwhelming. Still, it stabbed at my heart to make that phone call after having a frank discussion with my veterinarian days before. Even he was reluctant to do the deed at first. Like me, he, too, had observed the perseverance of these great horses coming through so much in the last few years, and we admired their spirit. We watched them enjoy each other's company like an old married couple. Standing in the casting shadow of Foxy's granite monument, it was time to choose a resting place for the horses. In this grief-filled decision, humour interrupted the mood when I insisted that Loli was to rest between her two boys. After all, Foxy would not tolerate another suitor taking up residence beside him.

Intrigue would go first. It was a sad farewell as I stole one last wistful look at him obediently and slowly walking down the road as the veterinarian led him to a place of eternal rest under the shade tree. For all that he was, Intrigue will be remembered for his nobility and blessed Morgan poise, intelligence, and independence.

Chapter 13

Shosholoza

Go Forward into Africa

In spring of 2006, my ailing mother asked me where I would like to go if I had to choose a place to visit. Without a second thought, I hastened to answer. Africa! My mother smiled and said to me, "I'll be with you in spirit, and you will go first class." A month later, she died in my arms, and my journey to Africa was a promise I would keep.

It was almost a year in the planning, but the day came when I would hitch a ride on a South African Airways flight to Johannesburg. It was to be a month-long adventure engaging in several safaris that would take me to four countries. I would have close encounters with all of Africa's Big Five and a few others. I would be chased by an elephant, ride an elephant, be challenged by a hippo, and witness a night kill on the grasslands of Kruger. On one of these safaris, I would arrive in Botswana and travel by bush plane and helicopter to a remote camp. I would ride the wild Okavango Delta on country-bred horses accustomed to the wicked terrain and dangerous predators. To put it mildly, it would be a trail ride to remember.

At each destination, I unpacked my duffle bag and placed Mother's photo by my crude nightstand. I was now alone, half a world away and sleeping in a tent with the haunting African wilds calling out in the darkness. I know Mother was watching over me, so I would have some help from a higher authority. No need to worry. *Just enjoy the experience,* I told myself.

The horses number fifty-six or so in herd size and stay in the open protection of the seasonal island 24/7, 365 days a year. A small, solar-powered electric strand of wire encloses them from the outside predators. Still, the odd crocodile will attempt to capture a horse at that water's edge, and some unfortunate horses bear the scars of their near mishap. That being said, these tough horses are very in tune with their environment and react swiftly to danger. Only proficient riders need apply on these riding treks.

Botswana safari

The days in saddle were long and dusty. In the winter season, the delta's clay soil turns to cement dust. Bone-dry bushes and sharp, cactus-like needles slashed across the protection of the leather leggings. I rode around the next bend in a never-ending, marauding game track. Occasionally, we stopped for lunch. The horses were tethered to a low bush as we rested beneath the shade of the huge sausage tree. After a short snack, we mounted up using the nearest log or termite mound. Then we were off again, heading home to an evening of gourmet native cooking while watching African television (the campfire). It was always an early night, as daybreak came soon enough with the call of the go-away bird as we mounted up again for another day on the delta.

It had been six days of challenging rides. Many included bareback riding, as the horses swam short waterways. We survived mad gallops racing alongside the striped cousin of the horse. We witnessed up close the bulldozers of Africa as the great elephants downed many trees with just a push from their mighty trunks. We sat silent and motionless while the fearless and short-tempered buffalos passed. I had a wrenched back, but a more serious peril awaited me.

My grey thoroughbred named Mazoozoo kept a steady pace with the six horses ahead of him while trotting head to tail following the lead horse. Dodging the razor-sharp bushes as we wound our way following the elephant trail, it seemed rather repetitive if not boring. Without warning, Mazoozoo dropped beneath me like a stone. His front hoof had found a burrowing hole, buckling him at the knee and tossing me forcefully to the hard clay. He stumbled and scrambled to right himself, seemingly unscathed with just a hint of lameness. I finally came to rest on my back, looking up at the clear African sky with excruciating pain emanating from the lower back.

I lay still. Cautiously, I willed my toes to move, and thankfully they responded. Little did I know at the time, but essentially, I had broken my back. It would not be diagnosed until my arrival back in Canada. Slowly, I made my way to my feet with a little assistance from the outriders and guide. It was the sort of pain that can only be expressed with an outpouring of tears. I bucked up and a short period later was eased into a military-style saddle where I could brace myself against the steel frame for support while partially standing in the stirrups. Since I would not be able to control the horse should danger present itself, the outrider with rifle in hand took the rein of my horse and became my bodyguard for the next while.

As we approached a small grove of trees, we momentarily startled a large herd of buffalo thrashing with panic in the thickets. These animals are aggressive and unafraid to challenge a lion or, in this case, a horse and incapacitated rider. The outrider did his best to keep my horse calm and hold his rifle and horse. It was at this point that I felt I may never see home again. If the buffalo charged us, I was dead! To everyone's relief, the herd rushed to the right of us. They were gone in a flash.

It would be a long, agonizing hour looking for a point in the watershed where a dugout canoe could make it in. With the aid of a two-way radio, help was on the way.

I was transferred to the dugout canoe. We navigated to deeper, more open water. From there, I struggled into an aluminum motor boat. At last in open water, the driver made speed while spooking a large male hippo that took a run at us. The hippo emerged out of the water like a huge rolling log just about 10 feet off our wake. Finally, a familiar sight lay ahead. The boat was brought to shore, and I was helped to my tent.

They had no ice packs other than those keeping the fish cool, so that had to do. Next, I asked for some horse liniment from the stable area, along with some horse bandages. It wouldn't be until late evening when a nurse who was visiting the camp would arrive. At least I was safe for the time being.

After a short visit with an English nurse who had finally landed at the camp and took all my insurance information and medical history, she informed me that it might be a while longer before they got back to me. You see, an elephant had wandered into the camp, and as it would happen, he decided he liked my tent area to poke around in as he grazed his way along.

As I held my breath with him trampling the vegetation outside, I thought I better make peace with God. The elephant sauntered off into the evening sunset, leaving me to my misery.

My premium travel insurance was proving to be worthless. A Medevac helicopter was the only way I could see out, but unless I had $5,000 in U.S. cash on me, it wasn't going to happen. And so there I lay in a canvas tent, half a world away with no visible way of leaving.

In the morning, a plan was hatched involving the only viable means of transporting me out. For two gruelling hours travelling at 10 km per hour, I lay on a mattress placed on the bed of a Land Rover truck. It bumped its way through brush, water, heat, and dust before rolling out on the grassy airstrip. From there, I was helped into the small Cessna for the flight to Maun.

As the plane landed and rolled its way along the tarmac to the ambulance, I was quickly assessed, and it was recommended that I fly directly back to Johannesburg.

As I waited in the lounge of the small international airport, I reached for my purse and passport. It had been taken from me and safely housed in the cab of the Land Rover while en route to the airstrip. My luggage had been unloaded from the plane minus my purse. The tour agent meekly told me that I would have to pay to have the plane go back and get my purse and that I might miss the only flight out of there.

I was quickly acquiring the temper of those wild buffalo. Shaking in pain, standing there with no passport, no credit cards, no money, no plane ticket, visas, etc., I was going to be the travel agent's worst nightmare since I was literally stranded. She followed my direction and sent the plane back, retrieved my purse, and asked officials to hold the plane. The lioness had won this round.

Asked if I would ever go back to Africa, my answer is *yes* in a heartbeat. For all the pain, drama, and wildness, there is nothing like the draw of its call. I just might not go on a horse.

Chapter 14

Full Circle

By the latter part of the 1980s, life on the farm was humming along with great gusto. Novelty ideas are always grandiose in thought, even if the final product would have to be scaled down considerably for reality's sake.

Ideas just seem to pop into my head without forewarning or planning. I suppose this inventive thought process was handed down by way of genes from my father and grandmother. I'm often compared to my father in this manner. I certainly frustrate many when they see that look I have and the enthusiasm that spills out of my mouth when I get one of those ideas. I am the inventor of my own imagination but don't always have the skill to deliver on these apparitions in my mind. I'm just the creative factor in the equation. That is where I depend on others to help see my projects through to fruition. Many don't know what they are getting themselves into as my ideas expand with explosive energy that sometimes surprises me. So was the case of the farm's Christmas festivals.

For a dozen years, the farm celebrated the Christmas season like no other stable. With each passing year, the farm's Christmas festival grew in attendance, imaginary design, and grandiosity. Media attention was widespread. It was always offered as a free event to the public. Everyone who walked through the main doors of the stable was encouraged to join in on the celebration. Every stall in the stable was decorated with a theme, and the entire barn (inside and out) received many festive touches, as well. More than 1,000 feet of fresh garland was trucked in from Nova Scotia to line the aisles of the stable. Those attending the open barn were handed a ballot and encouraged to vote for their favourite stall in several categories. Rosettes were presented to the winners based on the results of the nonpartisan public voting. By the last year of this mega event that was six months in the planning at that stage, a record 600 people walked through the doors of the stable on the afternoon of December 1. Busloads of holiday seekers disembarked from their rolling coaches. Poor Mother stood for hours with a space heater at her feet serving litre upon litre of hot apple cider, complements of the farm. The festival had grown too large to continue on a volunteer basis. It was no longer feasible to produce the festival as a free public relations event by drawing from the farm's meagre pennies; the financial burden was too great. Sadly, the festival had run its course.

To this day, many still recall the Christmas festivals of past years with fond smiles of acknowledgment and wonderment of how it all came together without a hitch.

Cranking out new programs and ideas has never been difficult for me. Not all my endeavours are successful. Perhaps it is just bad timing. Most inventive people are usually ahead of the times. My father was one of those people with forward thinking. It sometimes is a struggle to get these ideas off the ground. But I always go back to his words of wisdom, "Never stop dreaming. If you try long and hard enough to follow that dream, it will come true."

I have a yearning to share my knowledge and experience with others. I tend to be rather impulsive and passionate about lighting the way for others. We all have been novices at one time. No person has ever been born with the knowledge and experience that only time can impart on us. So with this in mind, I began to educate other horse people while continuing my own personal journey and thirst for knowledge through research, veterinary conventions, and general day-to-day experience.

The first of literally 100 or so workshops began in the back aisle of the barn with people resting their bones on hay bales and feverishly writing notes in their paperback journals sitting on their laps. These educational sessions were first offered at no charge to clients who had purchased a horse from us. My husband and I wanted to help ensure that these animals would be cared for in a knowledgeable and responsible family environment. And so it began one sunny Saturday afternoon in 1983. Since then, I have developed and presented workshops on numerous subjects. Many of these clinics had guest speakers, and all were professionals in their fields of expertise. People have attended from the far north in Ontario and many states below our border.

At the beginning of the millennium, I took early retirement from my civil servant post of twenty-two years with the provincial government. I literally went from my sedentary life at an office desk one morning to waking up the next and grabbing a pitchfork. There was no breather and no retirement. It was simply a direct, immediate lifestyle change. I have never regretted leaving the stuffy office chatter for the smell of manure and fresh hay. Nuts, you may say, but for those who were born to live on the land, we understand that calling of nature better than most, and I don't mean toilets.

The farm was now changing rapidly in direction. My breeding program was still in full swing with sales across Canada and exporting to the United States and Great Britain. My training program intensified, as well. Opportunities that only time could afford allowed me to start a lesson program on a grander scale than before. Still with the focus on education, I was quickly adapting my horse-training skills to create a unique lesson program for novice riders. It was not just the mechanics of riding I was teaching. I was also focusing more emphasis on the horse psychology that I had attained over the many years of working with and training horses. I wanted people to understand where the horse was coming from so that they could relate more effectively in their riding skills. This would be combined with the basic structure and foundation from contemporary riding programs.

I have always shied away from group lessons. I've been there as a youth rider and never found them that effective, especially those frustrated instructors that tend to yell and belittle. It is counterproductive and an insult to the riders' intelligence.

I enjoy engaging my students one-on-one, and that has been my style of teaching. Although it is not a great financial benefit for the farm, I get more personal satisfaction and reward from this form of coaching. Still, we all stumble in our efforts to teach everyone. It is always a learning curve trying to find the right communication avenue that a student can understand and process. But when it's achieved, it is glorious.

I've never been one to simply follow the crowd or fad. I sometimes challenge the conventional ways and pioneer other avenues. How boring life would be if we all followed the same river without discovering any of its tributaries.

I doubt it is a coincidence that a horse of Morgan heritage that strolled by my house on late afternoons when I was a young girl would have the same name as my Morgan foundation mare. Nor could it be a coincidence that I would establish a horse farm in the same area where my first horse, Magnificent, was foaled and purchased when I was just an awkward teen trying to adjust to life in southern Ontario. Call it fate or good karma. Whatever you believe, it was meant to be.

I take a little time these days to cater to my flock of exotic birds. I play with a pair of overweight and often mischievous goats that are mascots to the farm and simply love my dogs. The north and all of its rustic, wild beauty still beckons me each year. I suppose it will always be my home in the heart.

As the years imprint more wisdom and the aches of past bumps and thumps begin to rear in dull reminders of ancient misfortune, I cautiously continue to look ahead to the challenges of age while fighting resignation. Still, the mind continues to breathe new life into a sometimes waning body. Those people and memories of so long ago have enriched my life immeasurably.

I still feel the strong, gentle hand that led me to the bread wagon as a toddler when asked to see the Gee Gee. The old man in the stable never once questioned my ignorance and embarrassment for lack of knowledge but instead showed me how and encouraged me to try. If my years between the irons can bring that same level of confidence and pleasure to someone else, then I will have been successful. And as for the horses in my life, they are my life.